RAND PROJECT AIR FORCE

Strategic Warning on NATO's Eastern Flank

Pitfalls, Prospects, and Limits

Mark R. Cozad

Prepared for the United States Air Force
Approved for public release; distribution unlimited

For more information on this publication, visit www.rand.org/t/RR2080

Library of Congress Cataloging-in-Publication Data is available for this publication.
ISBN: 978-0-8330-9890-0

Published by the RAND Corporation, Santa Monica, Calif.

Preface

Since 2008, Russia's military has embarked on an extensive modernization program designed to overcome shortfalls in readiness, competence, sustainability, and deployability that impeded its operations in Chechnya and Georgia. Subsequent changes in logistics and operational capability have presented the intelligence community (IC) and decisionmakers with new challenges in warning about and responding to potential Russian aggression. Russian operations in Ukraine and Syria have demonstrated improved operational concepts and capabilities, including denial and deception activities and unconventional warfare designed to operate below U.S. and North Atlantic Treaty Organization (NATO) response thresholds; they are also intended to condition allied responses to new operational patterns and deployments. If successful, these activities could inhibit the IC's ability to assess Russia's intentions and courses of action within the timelines necessary for policymakers and military commanders to formulate effective responses.

Russia has been a relatively low priority for the IC since the end of the Cold War, as new security concerns and recent wars have dominated decisionmakers' attention, and the resources dedicated by both the IC and the military to warning of Russia's activities have diminished. However, warning in the Baltics became a major concern for both NATO and U.S. Air Force Europe in 2014, because of Russia's military operations and its continuing modernization efforts. This report assesses key elements of six Soviet and Russian actions to provide recommendations for improving warning of Russian military activities along NATO's eastern flank. It also considers the practical limits for what warning improvements can realistically provide and the implications these limitations have for U.S. and NATO decision timelines, force posture, and deterrence. The report should be of interest to military planners, foreign-policy experts concerned with European security, policymakers, intelligence professionals, and anyone interested in Russian and European security issues.

This research was conducted within the Strategy and Doctrine Program of RAND Project AIR FORCE as part of a fiscal year 2015 study, U.S. Airpower and Moscow's Emerging Strategy in the Near Abroad, sponsored by Headquarters United States Air Force in Europe, Directorate of Plans, Programs, and Analyses. Other unpublished RAND reports produced by this project are

- Bryan Frederick et al., "Assessing Russian Reactions to NATO Posture Enhancements," September 2016
- James Chow et al., "Assessing Options for Enhancing Airpower's Effectiveness in Defense of NATO's Eastern Flank," September 2016.

RAND Project AIR FORCE

RAND Project AIR FORCE (PAF), a division of the RAND Corporation, is the U.S. Air Force's federally funded research and development center for studies and analyses. PAF provides the Air Force with independent analyses of policy alternatives affecting the development, employment, combat readiness, and support of current and future air, space, and cyber forces. Research is conducted in four programs: Force Modernization and Employment; Manpower, Personnel, and Training; Resource Management; and Strategy and Doctrine. The research reported here was prepared under contract FA7014-06-C-0001.

Additional information about PAF is available on our web site:

http://www.rand.org/paf/

This report documents work originally shared with the U.S. Air Force on September 30, 2016. The draft report, issued in July 2016, was reviewed by formal peer reviewers and U.S. Air Force subject-matter experts.

Contents

(This page is intentionally blank.)

Summary

The relative priority of Russia as a national security concern has fallen substantially since the end of the Cold War. Accordingly, the Intelligence Community's (IC's) efforts to monitor Russia have declined, and more of its resources have been devoted to other concerns, such as Afghanistan, Iraq, global terrorism, China, and the Middle East. However, since 2008, Russia's military has embarked on an extensive modernization program designed to overcome the shortfalls in readiness, competence, sustainability, and deployability that impeded its operations in Chechnya and Georgia. Subsequent changes in logistics and operational capability have presented the IC and decisionmakers with new challenges in warning about and responding to potential Russian aggression. Russian operations in Georgia, Ukraine, and Syria have demonstrated improved operational concepts and capabilities, including denial and deception activities and unconventional warfare designed to operate below U.S. and North Atlantic Treaty Organization (NATO) response thresholds; they are also intended to condition allied responses to new operational patterns and deployments. If successful, these activities could inhibit the IC's ability to assess Russia's intentions and courses of action within the timelines necessary to formulate effective responses.

Providing warning of potential aggression by hostile nations has proven difficult for a variety of reasons, regardless of country or region. The difficulty of gaining insight into leadership intentions is a primary factor in this challenge. The limits to warning capabilities are magnified further by analyst and decisionmaker biases and a warning system that does not function consistently and may even present multiple assessments of the same situation from different organizations. In the end, warning is more art than science. Even when the warning system's elements work together effectively, it may be difficult to determine success or failure. A late or delayed decision from adversary leaders may confound warning and leave little time for U.S. and allied decisionmakers to respond. Moreover, a timely warning and response may change an enemy's behavior in ways that are not apparent to either the IC or decisionmakers, thus raising the prospect of the "cry wolf" syndrome or an alarmist IC.

Some decisionmakers, particularly within the Department of Defense, have raised concerns about the IC's ability to warn of future Russian activities in light of Russia's modernization and operations. Its reemergence as a national security priority stems from the potential for aggression on NATO's eastern flank and the corresponding threat posed to multiple NATO allies. In light of recent Russian operations and the uncertainty that accompanied them, U.S. decisionmakers are examining avenues for improving the IC's ability to provide timely warning of Russian aggression and coercion.[1]

[1] Sydney J. Freedberg, Jr., "Europe Needs Intel, Ships, & Focus: Gen. Breedlove," *Breaking Defense*, October 30, 2015; Jim Garamore, "Work Discusses Russia with Military, Intelligence Leaders," *DoD News*, *Defense Media*

Understanding Soviet and Russian leadership is a core challenge that complicates warning of potential Russian actions. This problem endures and compounds U.S. warning challenges because of Russia's geographic proximity to many of the areas where its forces have been committed or may be committed in the future. Other factors, such as denial and deception efforts and attempts to decrease U.S. and NATO sensitivity by routinizing military deployments and preparations, reduce the diagnostic value of indicators necessary for warning. These activities are designed to work together to impede or delay effective warning. With other high-priority issues competing for decisionmakers' attention and intelligence resources, the problem of potential Russian aggression against the Baltics is arguably the most challenging warning dilemma facing the IC and decisionmakers today.

This study examines six Soviet and Russian events that have occurred in the past 50 years that highlight some of these problems as they pertain to current concerns about aggression on NATO's eastern flank: (1) the Cuban missile crisis, (2) the Soviet invasion of Czechoslovakia, (3) the Soviet invasion of Afghanistan, (4) the Russian invasion of Georgia, (5) Russia's invasion of Crimea and operations in eastern Ukraine, and (6) Russia's deployment to Syria. Although some of these events, particularly Russia's invasion of Georgia and the three events that preceded it, have been characterized as warning failures, policymakers and the IC do not agree on the extent of the failures or their primary causes. Some senior government leaders have labeled the two most recent events—Russia's invasion of Crimea and its deployment to Syria—as failures, but others, including members of the White House staff and the Director of National Intelligence, did not see them as such.

This study does not provide a scorecard. It does not attempt to judge whether the IC warned successfully or failed in warning of the events considered. Nor does it attach blame to either policymakers or the IC. All too often, warning is treated as a binary issue and categorized as either a success or a failure. Many studies of warning assign blame to either the IC for missing key events and decisions or to policymakers for not acting upon an IC warning. The warning events highlighted in this study demonstrate that these clear-cut distinctions are often difficult, if not impossible, to make, and disagreements among an event's key participants often remain unresolved.

This report provides an overview of relevant factors in the selected warning events. It seeks to identify continuity in Russian operational practices and long-standing IC challenges that can be used to inform current efforts to improve warning. The report also addresses the many developments that have shaped warning since the fall of the Soviet Union and the beginning of Russia's military modernization efforts. These changes include major shifts in Russia's priority

---

Activity, April 17, 2015; Greg Miller, "As Russia Reasserts Itself, U.S. Intelligence Agencies Focus Anew on the Kremlin," *Washington Post*, September 1, 2016; Adam Entous, Julian E. Barnes, and Siobhan Gorman, "Without Warning: U.S. Scurries to Shore Up Spying on Russia," *Wall Street Journal*, March 24, 2014; Eli Dickey, Noah Lake, and Christopher Shachtman, "Ex-CIA Chief: Why We Keep Getting Putin Wrong," *Daily Beast*, March 2, 2014; Shane Harris, "Washington's Civil War over Russia Intel," *Daily Beast*, October 12, 2015; "Exclusive: Congress Probing U.S. Spy Agencies' Possible Lapses on Russia," Reuters, October 8, 2015.

for U.S. policymakers and the IC effort devoted to both warning in general and the Russian situation. This study identifies several themes concerning continuities and discontinuities and distills the findings into recommendations for improving Russia-related warning, primarily as it applies to NATO's eastern flank.

There is an extensive body of literature detailing the events examined in this study from a variety of perspectives, which have been used here to distill several themes. These themes identify areas where the IC has had success and areas where it has been challenged, including (1) Soviet/Russian conditioning of expectations through the use of exercises, (2) Soviet/Russian denial and deception, (3) the U.S. ability to monitor critical information and indicators, (4) U.S. inability to gain access to and misreading of Soviet/Russian intent, and (5) Soviet/Russian use of indirect action.

Russia's ability to condition expectations and implement denial and deception measures played a role in limiting decisionmakers' and the IC's understanding of leadership intent in each event. Furthermore, in several events, significant information and corresponding indicators were available, but Soviet and Russian intentions were unclear or misread. Indirect action—a strategy that attempts to neutralize enemy actions through the use of nonmilitary or unconventional warfare methods, including information warfare—was present in four of the six events, but it consistently has not provided diagnostic indicators that led to advanced warning of larger operations.[2] This does not mean that activities associated with indirect action will not provide diagnostic value for warning in the future. It only reflects how these activities were contextualized and understood for warning purposes in these events. In-depth research and analysis into indirect actions and their historical use may provide new insights relevant to improving warning.

Although the IC has fewer resources dedicated to Russia and the former Soviet Union than it had during the Cold War, in each of the events discussed in this report, the IC was able to monitor key activities that pointed to potential crisis. At no point was the IC surprised by a Soviet or Russian "bolt from the blue." In fact, the IC monitored force buildups, deployments, and readiness changes and was aware that Russian use of force was a possible course of action in each crisis. The key shortfall in each event was understanding Soviet and Russian leaders' intentions and identifying when those leaders finally decided to act. These two factors were generally not identified in time to permit decisionmakers to deter Soviet/Russian actions or respond immediately.

The themes identified in the warning events are not new, but they highlight the need for renewed emphasis on rebuilding expertise in this critical region, improving collection and analysis capabilities, and emphasizing key elements of analytic tradecraft that might improve warning. As Russia's relative priority within the IC evolves, the IC will face competing demands to support current intelligence and military planning. Actions necessary for warning frequently do

---

[2] Keir Giles, *Russia's "New Tools" for Confronting the West: Continuity and Innovation in Moscow's Exercise of Power*, London: Chatham House, The Royal Institute of International Affairs, March 21, 2016, p. 11.

not conform to immediate needs, so if improving warning is an actual priority, decisionmakers must ensure that the IC has adequate resources to rebuild the tools necessary for meeting this objective.

The insights derived from the examples presented here should help decisionmakers and commanders set boundaries for what they realistically can expect from warning. Even in cases where intelligence reporting and analysis are well-positioned, U.S. and NATO decisionmakers will frequently be faced with significant ambiguity. Delaying decisions for additional clarification or "unambiguous" warning will limit decision space and will consume much-needed time to develop and deploy options. Many of the Soviet/Russian decisions outlined in this study occurred late in a crisis. Knowing that this may well be the case in the future, decisionmakers and commanders will need to have war-gamed and considered potential outcomes and responses prior to the onset of crises in order to improve the possibility for a timely response.

Warning can be improved in several ways, including (1) rebuilding the IC's ability to provide in-depth coverage; (2) creating, utilizing, and maintaining improved warning indicators that cover both military and nonmilitary activities; (3) developing focused training for IC collectors and analysts, particularly in warning tradecraft and adversary denial and deception practices; (4) building and leveraging experience and expertise within and outside of the IC; (5) increasing research into how Russia transitions its military, economy, and population from peace to war.

Improvement will not be a short-term endeavor. Any success that emerges from implementing these recommendations will require time and vision. In scenarios like the situation in the Baltics, the gains derived from improved warning likely will not be enough to enable immediate responses to Russian operations. This highlights a core element of the warning dilemma: In the absence of in-depth analysis, experience, and adequate resources, warning failure is a high-probability outcome, if not a near certainty. Even with significant resources, deep understanding of the target, and a well-developed system, warning is often contingent upon access to information on adversary intent, which generally is opaque and often changes as leaders reevaluate the overall situation and the courses of action available to them. Thus, while improvements in analysis and collection will guard against outright failure, they will not guarantee success.

Warning is not solely an intelligence function. Policymakers can contribute to improving the warning process in several ways, including (1) communicating more-clearly-defined priorities, (2) setting and maintaining realistic expectations for what warning can provide in the policy process, and (3) considering and developing realistic options prior to actual crises. Warning is essential for both providing the time necessary to make decisions and the quality of the decisions ultimately made. Less time and poor information are likely to have direct, negative effects on crisis decisionmaking.

Effective warning requires active engagement by all the decisionmakers involved. Improved warning will do little if the will and resources necessary for an appropriate response are not present. In some of the events studied here, e.g., the Soviet invasion of Czechoslovakia, even if policymakers had received what they would categorize as adequate warning, it is unclear what practical options were available. Today, this is true regarding NATO's eastern flank. Without an increase in the overall force posture and readiness to respond in the event of Russian aggression, improved warning will have little positive overall effect. It cannot make up for a perceived lack of will or an inability to respond because of resource constraints. The time between a Russian decision and the beginning of an operation could be short—as analysis of earlier events suggests, it could be as little as two weeks or even less. As Russia continues to improve the speed with which it can mobilize and deploy its forces, these timelines are likely to become shorter. In areas where there is already an overwhelming Russian advantage, increased warning lead times will be highly unlikely, and marginal improvements in warning will offer little value to policymakers and commanders. Bolstering the U.S. and NATO posture will remain the best option for deterring future Russian aggression in the Baltics.

(This page is intentionally blank.)

Acknowledgments

This report would not have been possible without the contribution of two RAND colleagues who were instrumental in the report's conceptual development and in conducting the research that underpins its central findings. Brien Alkire provided the initial guidance and thinking, based on his recent work supporting Air Force intelligence. He spent considerable time conceptualizing and framing the key warning challenges for both collection and analysis. His insights were particularly valuable in identifying areas of concern for the project's sponsors. Balys Gintautas provided extensive and detailed analysis of the events analyzed in the report. His careful research and attention to detail illuminated several key issues that cut across the six events.

The thorough reviews provided by Roger George and Rich Girven added considerably to the final report. Both reviewers were able to help clarify and strengthen several of its key arguments and conclusions. The benefit of their extensive experience in the intelligence community added greatly to the final report.

(This page is intentionally blank.)

Abbreviations

CIA	Central Intelligence Agency
COA	course of action
DCI	Director of Central Intelligence
DCID	Director of Central Intelligence Directive
DoD	Department of Defense
IC	Intelligence Community
ICD	Intelligence Community Directive
NATO	North Atlantic Treaty Organization
NIE	National Intelligence Estimate
NIO-W	National Intelligence Officer for Warning
RFAF	Russian Federation Armed Forces
SNIE	Special National Intelligence Estimate

(This page is intentionally blank.)

1. Introduction: The Warning Dilemma

Since the Intelligence Community's (IC's)[1] inception, warning has been one of its highest priorities. However, the IC has had to balance multiple competing priorities to identify and monitor enduring and emerging threats to U.S. national security. Recognizing the need to prevent surprise attacks, its foremost function has been and remains alerting U.S. and allied leaders of potential dangers. Over the course of its existence, the IC has generally been successful; however, some notable failures have led senior policymakers and IC leaders to periodically reexamine, reassess, and reorient the IC's organization, resources, and priorities in light of emerging threats, changes in the security environment, and shifting policy priorities.[2] A prominent example of the IC's introspection into and reform of its warning structure resulted from its failure to warn of Iraq's 1991 invasion of Kuwait.[3] Immediately following that invasion, the Director of Central Intelligence (DCI) established a task force to examine the IC's organization and practices for providing warning. The task force also provided recommendations on how warning should be performed in the future to meet policymakers' needs in an international environment that would be vastly different from the Cold War alignment that had long defined U.S. policy and intelligence focus.[4]

As priorities and requirements have changed over time, the IC has reoriented its limited resources to focus on what policymakers have identified as their most pressing needs. These

[1] The IC comprises all analysts, managers, and senior leaders within the 16 U.S. government agencies that conduct intelligence activities and the military departments.

[2] There is an extensive literature on the IC's approach to warning over the years. Some of the most useful sources on how these changes shaped that approach are John F. McCreary, "Warning Cycles," *Studies in Intelligence*, Vol. 27, No. 3, Fall 1983, p. 71; Mary O. McCarthy, "The National Warning System: Striving for an Elusive Goal," *Defense Intelligence Journal*, Vol. 3, 1994, pp. 5–19; Charles E. Allen, "Warning and Iraq's Invasion of Kuwait: A Retrospective Look," *Defense Intelligence Journal*, Vol. 7, No. 2, 1998, pp. 33–44; Cynthia Grabo, "The Watch Committee and the National Indications Center: The Evolution of U.S. Strategic Warning 1950–1975," *International Journal of Intelligence and Counterintelligence*, Vol. 3, No. 3, 1989, pp. 363–385. While this list is by no means exhaustive, it provides a starting point for examining the literature produced by notable members of the IC's warning community.

[3] See DCI, *DCI Task Force Report: Improving Intelligence Warning*, May 29, 1992, approved for public release April 25, 2012, p. 2. This report noted that "except for the priority requirement of a military attack on the U.S. or its allies by the former Soviet Union, the National Intelligence Community has never seriously attempted to establish dedicated analytical programs for intelligence warning on a global scale." The report identified continued difficulties with the IC's organization despite previous efforts outlining organizational responsibilities (p. 4), and it contended that for warning, "no such 'system' currently exists and the National Warning System is more of an illusion than a reality."

[4] See DCI, 1992, p. 4.

shifts have at times entailed accepting increased risk in order to balance resources among competing demands.

The reform efforts highlight the dilemma that faces policymakers and IC leaders: In the absence of in-depth analysis, experience, and adequate resources, the probability of warning failure increases. As policymaker priorities adapt to new threats and concerns, the IC must ensure that it meets decisionmakers'[5] dynamic needs. The DCI task-force report and subsequent studies of warning have demonstrated that this requires the IC to shift its collection and analysis resources to areas that may have received limited attention in the past.[6] As priorities among intelligence targets change, collection requirements and capabilities change and analysts are asked to reorient their efforts. This dynamic landscape requires adaptable people and capabilities, conceivably at the expense of tailored collection efforts and regional expertise. Reconstituting these capabilities can be difficult and costly, and it is unlikely to be accomplished quickly.

Timely warning is often contingent upon access to information on opaque adversary intent that can change as foreign leaders reevaluate the overall situation and the courses of action (COAs) available to them. Building or rebuilding the capabilities necessary to provide timely warning generally requires a mix of additional resources, collection capabilities, and analytic expertise. These are not acquired quickly or without cost. The dilemma is that while the improvements will decrease the likelihood of outright failure, they will not guarantee success. The problem relates not only to cost-benefit factors of investing in improved warning capability, but also to the core issue of how decisionmakers and the IC define success and failure. In situations where early warning is received and decisionmakers have time to react, an adversary may modify its behavior and decide against taking immediate action. In such cases, a warning success may never be known—the situation may appear to be one where the IC "cried wolf."[7] Repeated warnings over time may also desensitize decisionmakers who believe that the adversary has not taken action. And while decisionmakers seek "early" warning, an adversary's leaders may not make a final decision until relatively late in a crisis, thus limiting the ability to respond even if the IC is able to warn at the time of the adversary's decision. Potentially costly and time-intensive efforts to build warning capabilities still may not be able to provide warning in enough time for decisionmakers to act.

---

[5] In this report, decisionmakers include senior officials in policy roles across the government, commanders, and military planners.

[6] Mary O. McCarthy, "The Mission to Warn: Disaster Looms," *Defense Intelligence Journal*, Vol. 7, No. 2, 1998; McCarthy, 1994, pp. 5–19; Science Applications International Corporation, *Warning in Uncertainty—Rethinking Warning in a Changing World*, conference summary, Herndon, Va., February 1, 2000; John A. Kringen, "Rethinking the Concept of Global Coverage in the U.S. Intelligence Community," *Studies in Intelligence*, Vol. 59, No. 3, September 2015.

[7] McCreary, 1983, p. 75.

Warning About the Soviet Union and Russia: Then and Now

One of the DCI task force's major findings was that the IC needs to focus on concerns that go beyond major conventional conflict and political instability in key states.[8] In response to policymakers' needs to address a host of new problems, including ethnic unrest, counternarcotics, and genocide, the IC shifted a significant part of its focus to identifying potential regional dynamics that might involve or threaten U.S. resources and personnel (e.g., in Somalia, Bosnia, West Africa, and Iraq). Concurrently, many of the capabilities directed toward the former Soviet Union were reoriented to other intelligence problems. Over time, the IC was given far fewer resources with which to monitor developments in Russia.

The warning evolution that occurred after the end of the Cold War underpins several major themes in this study. First, the expertise and understanding of Soviet military planning and the capabilities necessary for producing assessments required extensive time and resources to develop. These capabilities did not materialize on short notice, and the number and experience level of analysts dedicated to this central problem had grown significantly over time. The IC was able, over the course of long analysis, to obtain a deep level of understanding facilitated by extensive collection resources and guided by the wide-ranging expertise of analysts dedicated to the core warning problem of the day.[9]

The second theme involves the level of attention U.S. political and military leaders devoted to Russian activities as a matter of course during the Cold War. An extensive portion of the U.S. policy community and much of the military were focused on missions that in some way or another involved countering or deterring the Soviet Union or its allies. Thus, those responsible for responding to crises understood the problem and were supported by a force posture that provided significant response options.

A third theme is that regardless of how much expertise and attention was devoted to the problems of Cold War warning, the IC and policy communities had only limited understanding of Soviet intentions. This limitation became evident during several crises, including the Cuban missile crisis, the Soviet invasion of Czechoslovakia, and the Soviet invasion of Afghanistan. The same lack of understanding has figured prominently in more-recent Russian actions in Georgia, Ukraine, and Syria. Its relevance remains and must be taken into account as the IC explores the steps it can take today to improve its warning capabilities against Russia.

In spite of the critical lack of understanding of Soviet leaders' intentions, the United States had well-developed indicator lists and significant amounts of quality intelligence on Soviet force posture that indicated when there was a potential for hostilities. The IC closely monitored and

---

[8] The report termed these traditional focus areas as "big W" types of warning problems.

[9] For an excellent example of the level of analysis dedicated to Russia's actions at an early date, see Thomas J. Patton, "The Monitoring of War Indicators," *Studies in Intelligence*, Vol. 3, Winter 1959, declassified September 18, 1995, p. 57 (part of Record Group 263 in "Records of the Central Intelligence Agency, 1894–2002," National Archives at College Park, Md.). Later examples include DCI, *Warning of War in Europe: Changing Warsaw Pact Planning and Forces*, Memorandum to Holders, NIE 4-1-84, September 1989.

reported on events in great detail as they progressed, and it placed even greater focus on events once they began to unfold. In none of the major crises was the community caught completely off guard. However, there was only limited direct intelligence on Soviet or Russian leadership intentions,[10] and in several cases, intelligence analysts and policymakers did not agree on whether appropriate warning had been delivered.[11] In other situations, policymakers delayed making decisions until they felt they had a sufficient level of certainty. The examples in this study demonstrate that effective warning is not merely the sum of a series of well-defined parts. Effective warning also generally cannot alleviate shortfalls in force posture and realistic policy options. If forces and planning are not in place and aligned to respond effectively, warning becomes an informational exercise. Warning should, therefore, always be thought of in the context of time requirements as time relates to leadership decisions, whether those decisions are being made by our adversaries or by our own leaders.

Background

Russian military operations since 2008 and more-recent "no-notice" military exercises that the Russian Federation Armed Forces (RFAF) reinstituted in 2013 have raised concerns among senior U.S. and North Atlantic Treaty Organization (NATO) leaders that the IC's ability to warn of Russian aggression has atrophied. This perceived shortcoming is seen as presenting significant risk to alliance leaders charged with protecting NATO's eastern flank from future Russian military actions. Questions about the IC's warnings of Russian military operations in Georgia, Crimea, eastern Ukraine, and Syria all contribute to an overarching concern among senior U.S. commanders that the IC's ability to warn of future Russian actions is seriously challenged.[12] In view of Russia's significant efforts to address operational shortcomings highlighted in earlier events and an increasingly provocative and aggressive posture toward U.S. and NATO forces in the region, these concerns call into question NATO's ability to deter or respond in a timely fashion to Russian aggression. Russian leaders seem to possess a highly centralized decisionmaking process that enables them to operate within the U.S. and NATO decision cycle. Furthermore, Russia's physical proximity to potential conflict zones and the increased size and

---

[10] For a recent example, see Eli Dickey, Noah Lake, and Christopher Shachtman, "Ex-CIA Chief: Why We Keep Getting Putin Wrong," *Daily Beast*, March 2, 2014. For historical examples, see Central Intelligence Agency (CIA), *Strategic Warning & the Role of Intelligence: Lessons Learned from the 1968 Soviet Invasion of Czechoslovakia*, Center for the Study of Intelligence, 2010; Donald P. Steury, ed., *Sherman Kent and the Board of National Estimates: Collected Essays*, Washington, D.C.: CIA, Center for the Study of Intelligence, 1994, pp. 175–188.

[11] This study does not attempt to adjudicate these disagreements. Several press articles, interviews, and scholarly studies (including some by the IC) acknowledge disagreements about the effectiveness of warning in Czechoslovakia, Afghanistan, Georgia, and Ukraine.

[12] These concerns are discussed in Aaron Mehta, "Gen. Breedlove: Intelligence Community Changing How It Handles Russia," *Defense News*, October 30, 2015; "Congress Probing U.S. Spy Agencies' Possible Lapses on Russia," *World News*, October 7, 2015.

improved readiness of its military provide it with many options that can be executed relatively quickly.[13]

This report assesses the challenges facing the IC and decisionmakers, particularly in providing advance notice of a major Russian military operation on NATO's eastern flank. It also presents recommendations for improving shortfalls in existing capabilities. These recommendations are based on analysis of previous IC warning efforts that have had demonstrated success, particularly in cases where a target nation attempted to condition U.S. or allied responses or conduct denial and deception activities. The recommendations also urge senior policymakers and intelligence leaders to consider potential warning-posture tradeoffs and the extent to which early warning is an actual priority, as opposed to merely a stated priority.[14]

Warning is not solely an intelligence function—it requires active engagement on the part of policymakers and military commanders. Richard Betts, in a study on surprise attacks and their implications for military posture and planning, stated, "The common view is that surprise occurs because intelligence services fail to warn."[15] However, in many situations, "leaders in the victim state were warned that the enemy was marshalling the capabilities to strike but they did not react to the warning in ways that hindsight demonstrates were necessary." The tendency, he argued, is to place the emphasis on warning and detection rather than response. In circumstances where warning needs improvement, reliance on it might create a sense of overconfidence that carries with it severe risks and potential consequences. The present study also addresses the limits of warning and the expectations that are reasonable when considering options to improve it.

Policymakers and military leaders who are the recipients of warning must ask the broader question: What constitutes successful warning? Each of the warning events involving the Soviet Union or Russia examined in this report raises questions about whether better policy responses could have been crafted if policymakers were given additional time. Was there sufficient time to craft a response or to gain acceptance among all the necessary alliance members or interested parties? Were the necessary forces and resources in locations that would enable a timely response? As these questions suggest, detection is only the initial point in this process. Warning and response are, by necessity, inextricably tied.

---

13 These short timelines are highlighted in David A. Shlapak and Michael W. Johnson, *Reinforcing Deterrence on NATO's Eastern Flank: Wargaming the Defense of the Baltics*, Santa Monica, Calif.: RAND Corporation, RR-1253-A, 2016.

14 A stated goal is a desired endpoint toward which a specific system is oriented. However, the system may not have the requisite structure and resources to actually attain that goal. In this report, an actual goal of warning is to ensure that resources and structure are oriented to those tasks that are deemed most significant for improving warning on a regular basis. The distinction between stated and actual priorities is important when weighing the demand for current intelligence against intelligence resources devoted to in-depth research. See Russell Ackoff, "Towards a System of System Concepts," *Management Science*, Vol. 17, No. 11, July 1971, pp. 661–671; C. Argyris, *Knowledge for Action: A Guide to Overcoming Barriers to Operational Change*, San Francisco: Jossey-Bass, 1993.

15 Richard K. Betts, *Surprise Attack: Lessons for Defense Planning*, Washington, D.C.: Brookings Institution Press, 1982, p. 16.

Approach of This Study

This report relies heavily on historical sources and current press reporting for identifying and examining prominent themes in the context of current U.S. and NATO warning capabilities. Its conclusions are derived from several sources, including declassified intelligence assessments, historical studies of strategic warning and surprise, recent press reporting, war games that examine potential Russian COAs on NATO's eastern flank, and recent studies on Russia's military modernization. Warning is examined not only as a methodological and functional process, but also as a cognitive process in which decisionmakers receiving warning and the analysts providing it frame their analyses and decisions based on analogies, perceptions, and conceptual models. By identifying and understanding how these factors influenced previous events, we can determine the relative and practical limits of innovative strategies for enhancing warning.

The warning events examined in this study are not judged as successes or failures. Members of the IC and the decisionmakers with whom they serve are often at odds over the details of events: What information was available? When were key pieces of analysis prepared? When were they presented? Who received them and did they clearly warn? Adjudicating which view is correct is a historical endeavor heavily shaped by the perceptions of the actors involved. A simple examination of the record is unlikely to tell the entire story, and relying on the experiences and memory of key players can at times be problematic. Likewise, simply deferring to decisionmaker prerogatives may gloss over problems in the U.S. ability to respond and the constraints that led to those problems. One former senior IC official argued that the IC had done an adequate job of warning in the case of Russia's invasion of Georgia; however, a senior policy customer did not have the same view.[16]

The outputs from the warning process must be understood within the broader context of warning as it has evolved following the end of the Cold War. Since 2010, the IC has undergone several organizational changes in the way it addresses warning, in particular, the disestablishment of the National Intelligence Officer for Warning (NIO-W) position and the National Intelligence Managers' assumption of warning responsibilities in their respective regional or functional areas.[17] This report does not discuss recent organizational developments in the U.S. warning system; however, it explores elements of the system to determine whether historical shortcomings were episodic or an inherent part of the warning business.[18] Generally, we consider how warning is delivered at an institutional level, with relatively limited insight into

[16] Interview with a former senior IC official.

[17] The NIO-W position was instituted by DCI Directive in 1979 (DCI, Directive No. 1/5, *National Intelligence Warning*, May 23, 1979 [document superseded DCID No. 1/5, effective May 18, 1976]). This directive laid out the organizational construct for the National Intelligence Warning System and defined the NIO-W's responsibilities.

[18] Additional details on how warning is managed within the IC are given in Mark Cozad, "Strategic Warning: Organizing and Managing the Mission for the Current Era," Santa Monica, Calif.: RAND Corporation, unpublished.

the analytic processes that lead to outcomes.[19] Because only limited information is available on how analysts made assessments and the factors that shaped their perspectives, we relied on the analytic products, with limited understanding of the specific perceptions and editorial judgments that shaped these products. However, understanding how the broader intelligence and warning processes shape analyst and policymaker approaches to warning-related issues would help to identify ways to improve U.S. warning capabilities.

Finally, the study examines the Soviet/Russian events in the context of the warning-response dynamic that Betts and other authors have highlighted.[20] Renewed efforts to improve warning of Russian aggression should take advantage of the knowledge gained from earlier events. This study highlights several contextual differences in these events that should shape recommendations for the future. It raises questions about what the IC is being asked to provide as warning—mere detection or something more? Recent Russian operations in Georgia and Ukraine have highlighted the speed with which Russian actions have occurred or might occur in the future. They have also demonstrated a series of complex problems associated with potential U.S. and NATO responses, including current force posture, logistics, and alliance participation.[21] Reflecting the information provided in this body of work, this study provides a realistic baseline regarding what policymakers and military commanders should expect from the IC in terms of warning.

Organization of the Report

Chapter 2 addresses past approaches of policymakers and planners to warning and how the IC structures warning problems. As the IC rebuilds its capacity for providing analysis on major conventional threats and great-power competitors, it will be necessary to identify the strengths and weaknesses of traditional approaches and methodologies, rather than simply applying historical examples to future events without considering the ways an adversary like Russia is evolving. It is also necessary to understand where the historical methodologies have fallen short before any practical and workable solutions can be considered.

---

19 Analytic bias is a major factor contributing to intelligence failures. Over the years, the IC has attempted to mitigate this bias through the use of structured analytic techniques and the development of analytic standards across agencies (see Richards J. Heuer, Jr., *Psychology of Intelligence Analysis*, Washington, D.C.: CIA, Center for the Study of Intelligence, 1999; Richards J. Heuer, Jr., and Randolph H. Pherson, *Structured Analytic Techniques for Intelligence Analysis*, Washington, D.C.: CQ Press College, 2010; Director of National Intelligence, *Intelligence Community Directive 203: Analytic Standards*, January 2, 2015). These practices have been adopted widely within the IC, except in the State Department Office of Intelligence and Research. However, to date, there has been no systematic study of whether they have improved analysis (see Stephen Artner, Rich Girven, and James Bruce, *Assessing the Value of Structured Analytic Techniques in the U.S. Intelligence Community*, Santa Monica, Calif.: RAND Corporation, RR-1408-OSD, 2016).

20 Betts, 1982; Richard K. Betts, "Surprise Despite Warning: Why Sudden Attacks Succeed," *Political Science Quarterly*, Vol. 95, No. 4, December 1980.

21 Shlapak and Johnson, 2016.

Chapter 3 presents key warning themes from six events—three involving the Soviet Union and three involving Russia. These themes highlight similarities and contrasts in the crises. They show what the IC was able to provide, where it fell short, and key variables that contributed to failures in each case. They also highlight indirectly the different priorities and resources devoted to understanding Soviet or Russian capabilities and intent. While these examples may not at first seem to be connected, the themes demonstrate that certain problems persist regardless of the resources devoted to the target.

Chapter 4 details recommendations for improving warning on NATO's eastern flank, with a primary focus on the warning-response dynamic. It examines the extent to which warning can meet the demands being placed on it and whether improvements—even substantial ones—will be capable of providing policymakers and commanders with the time necessary to develop and implement effective COAs. It also offers several considerations for policymakers and commanders regarding priorities, expectations, and the need to have realistic options that can be executed on short notice if necessary.

Chapter 5 presents the conclusions of the study.

2. Warning Pitfalls

To evaluate current U.S. warning capabilities, it is necessary to clearly define *warning* and its associated functions. Warning is often discussed as an intelligence function, with attention placed primarily on the quality of collection and analysis, as viewed against the timeliness and accuracy of the disseminated outputs. This view fails to address the importance of decisionmaking and its resultant actions in formulating appropriate responses to warnings. The emphasis on the IC's role and the extent to which the IC satisfied or failed to meet policymakers' needs for warning in a particular event implies that timely warning is a necessary precursor to a policy response.

However, this approach does not account for the limits of what warning can provide and the corresponding difficulties that lead policymakers to delay their decisions in the hope of added clarity, certainty, or decision space. Furthermore, it fails to address the resource restrictions that affect the range of options available. Several historical examples demonstrate that strategic surprise often results from policymakers delaying their decisions or failing to respond to developments preceding an event.[1] To place warning in the broader context of U.S. and NATO force posture on NATO's eastern flank, this study focuses on the limitations of warning that policymakers and commanders should expect and what these limitations imply for responding to Russian aggression.

Warning is a process comprising two components, one involving intelligence alerts and the other involving policy decisions and responses.[2] Thus, the primary challenge should be defined as a warning-response problem, in which intelligence notification of an impending adversary action is a necessary first step but by no means an end in itself.[3]

This chapter outlines the first component of the problem—alerting and warning—by describing how the community has historically defined warning problems and the methodologies

---

[1] Betts, 1982, p. 123; Ephraim Kam, *Surprise Attack: The Victim's Perspective*, Cambridge, Mass.: Harvard University Press, 1988, p. 2; Richard K. Betts, "Analysis, War, and Decision: Why Intelligence Failures Are Inevitable," *World Politics*, Vol. 31, No. 1, October 1978. Betts, in particular, highlights several instances in the post–World War II era when policy decisions were delayed because of preconceptions about enemy capabilities, desires to pursue diplomatic outcomes, deception, and other factors. One example is the Israeli Ministry of Defense's willingness to ignore the reinforcement and redeployment of Egyptian forces—a factor that invalidated the key Israeli planning assumption that the Israeli Defense Force could achieve a favorable force ratio with its own mobility prior to an Arab attack. According to Betts, information that contradicts prevailing perspectives, particularly those most central to major policies, must satisfy a significantly higher burden of proof to gain acceptance.

[2] Betts, 1980, p. 552; McCreary, 1983, p. 72.

[3] Alexander L. George and Jane E. Holl, *The Warning-Response Problem and Missed Opportunities in Preventive Diplomacy*, New York: Carnegie Commission on Preventing Deadly Conflict, Carnegie Corporation of New York, 1997.

it has employed to deal with them. This information was derived primarily through identifying and monitoring key indicators in theoretical scenarios or actual events. From a warning perspective, much of the IC's warning effort has been devoted to collecting and analyzing information related to these indicators. The chapter next examines the IC's traditional approach to warning in general and then considers the implications for policymakers and commanders concerned with warning against Russian actions in particular.

The Traditional Warning Approach

Traditional warning methodologies have focused primarily on using indicators—"known or theoretical step[s] which the adversary should or may take in preparation for hostilities"[4]—to identify significant changes in an enemy's posture that might signal specific threats. Generally, indicators reflect prevailing models or scenarios for specific actions an adversary may take prior to and at the outset of hostilities. These "working hypotheses about reality" form the cornerstone for perceiving "change and discontinuity, in contrast to continuous and 'normal' evolutionary sequences."[5] Each indicator ideally represents a discrete, identifiable action that, when considered along with other indicators, might provide analysts with a body of activities that signify a materializing threat.

The IC has traditionally assumed that timely warning relies on the need to understand both capabilities and intentions. This line of thinking holds that to develop quality indicators, analysts must have insight into the types, numbers, and characteristics of an adversary's order of battle and key weapons systems. Understanding logistics and sustainment capacity, particularly as they relate to the types of forces in a particular military, can provide analysts with an understanding of how long forces might be able to operate at particular distances. Similarly, identifying mobility and transportation capabilities can enable analysts to bound potential operating areas and develop timelines for the length of time it will take to get forces to their necessary locations. Finally, understanding an adversary's command-and-control equipment and architecture (e.g., levels of control, degrees of autonomy, and targeting capacity) can enable analysis of the types of operations the adversary is likely to pursue.

Identifying technical capabilities, deployments, and numbers is not sufficient, however, for creating the scenarios needed to develop indicators of a particular course of action (COA). Simply focusing on capabilities for any military runs the risk of reinforcing biases or making incorrect assumptions about the types of risks adversary leaders are willing to take. Additionally, a capabilities-centric outlook may ignore other pressures driving those leaders toward actions that use their military forces in unexpected ways. Therefore, warning analysis has also

---

[4] Cynthia M. Grabo, *Anticipating Surprise: Analysis for Strategic Warning*, Bethesda, Md.: Center for Strategic Intelligence Research, Joint Military Intelligence College, 2002, p. 3.

[5] McCreary, 1983, p. 72.

emphasized understanding an adversary's intentions, through either direct or indirect means. Direct means include reporting about the deliberations and outcomes of adversary leadership meetings and decisionmaking processes. Such reporting on a regular, sustained basis is often beyond the IC's capabilities and access. Indeed, there is no indication that the IC had access to this type of information in any of the six events examined in this study.

Indirect reporting comes from sources such as war plans, doctrine, and exercises. Each of these sources is limited in its ability to provide insight into intentions. Understanding doctrine might provide the framework for understanding how an adversary might employ its capabilities under different conditions,[6] and insight into war plans and the planning process might provide a clear connection into how a military would prepare and deploy for military operations once leaders have decided upon putting a plan into action. However, these types of evidence do not provide any clarity on the decision to exercise or implement them. Although indirect means of understanding intentions require significant effort, they are probably more attainable than gaining access to sensitive leadership deliberations. Monitoring capabilities and intentions provides the baseline for setting the parameters of a war problem, but the effort to define warning problems faces two challenges that go beyond the capabilities and intentions framework. These challenges concern the issue of how a nation goes to war.[7] The first challenge is the extent to which IC analysts have considered the range of options available to an adversary and their understanding of that adversary's decisionmaking processes and central motivations. Understanding capabilities and intentions may allow analysts to draw conclusions about plausible scenarios, but the scenarios developed by this process may conform to the analysts' own biases. Accordingly, where possible, scenarios should be developed in light of an adversary's doctrine, war planning, and exercise activities.[8] Integrating this information requires long-term research. Doctrine typically is not static, particularly in the case of the Russian military. It adapts on the basis of perceived changes in the international security environment and developing trends in warfare. Awareness of these evolutions and the perceptions that underpin them should also be considered in the context of military exercises and planning.[9] Integrating this broad body of analysis can be challenging, particularly since analysts working on doctrine and strategy issues are often focused on long-term research and less connected with current intelligence reporting. To effectively define a warning problem and the likely scenarios that it entails, the IC must dedicate resources to such long-term research and routinely use it to inform current intelligence analysis.[10]

---

[6] Grabo, 2002, pp. 17–20.

[7] Grabo, 2002, p. 53. This subject is briefly discussed in Allen, 1998, pp. 33–36.

[8] Grabo, 2002, p. 53.

[9] Grabo, 2002, p. 54.

[10] Grabo argues that analysts working on long-term issues, particularly doctrine and strategy, are not the same analysts who produce current intelligence products (Grabo, 2002, p. 54). The division between long-term and

Doctrinal materials generally present discussions of operational military issues. However, nonmilitary preparations for war must also be considered in scenario development. During the 1980s, a significant amount of work detailed preparations that nations with planned economies—including the Soviet Union, North Korea, Syria, Iraq, and India—took to prepare for war.[11] The findings demonstrated that these nations began their preparations by diverting resources from the civilian economy toward the military. These diversions required governments to manage a range of activities that cut across their nations' social, political, economic, and military life.[12] Legal guidelines, regulations, and mobilization procedures are still integral to understanding how foreign leaders contemplating military action envision the threats and contingencies for which they have to plan. Mobilization exercises and related activities may be key elements of this process, but they do not provide a comprehensive understanding of the full scope of activities or the legal, regulatory, and procedural challenges involved. These nonmilitary factors are essential for creating scenarios and developing indicators, because they represent a set of activities that can disrupt the economy and lead to internal unrest if not managed effectively. Identifying nonmilitary preparations may help bound the types of scenarios leaders consider and the types of operations they undertake, particularly when faced with an adversary capable of escalating the conflict.

The second difficulty in analyzing how a country goes to war is based on the IC's knowledge and understanding of how an adversary operates on a routine basis. As capabilities develop, routine operations likely will reflect new operational concepts and tactics designed around them. Similarly, adversaries also evaluate and reassess the international security environment, often seeking to identify new methods of warfare. Their assessments may also lead to changes in leadership intent as new opportunities or threats emerge and others recede. As a result, the routine operations of an adversary, particularly Russia, will adapt to new conditions. Identifying norms in activity requires long-term research and may involve historical analysis in areas where the IC has retained limited experience or expertise in its analytic workforce. Furthermore, routine operations must be constantly reevaluated in ways beyond current intelligence reporting. Specific warning problems and their associated scenarios should be dynamic and should incorporate new developments. In some cases, threats may remain fixed for relatively long time periods (e.g., North Korea, the Taiwan Strait, and Cold War Europe); however, competing territorial claims and the emergence—in some cases, re-emergence—of major powers creates a dynamic environment that challenges the IC's ability to define warning problems and keep them current. It is thus a challenge for the IC to continuously evaluate the norms on which to base its warning

---

current intelligence is well documented and acknowledged by many in the IC. The present author's discussions with intelligence professionals in the IC and his own experience provide numerous examples of this division.

[11] Allen, 1998, p. 35.

[12] Grabo, 2002, p. 55.

scenarios and indicators to distinguish between routine activity and anomalous patterns that may portend a specific threat to national interests.

Warning intelligence also requires dynamism, which includes collecting new types of sources that go beyond traditional intelligence reporting on military activities and incorporates sources on legal, doctrinal, and procedural developments. Dynamism also entails developing a long-term research effort that enables analysts to more readily identify changes that fall outside areas they traditionally monitor and incorporate new findings into diagnostic indicators that may better reflect leadership intent and preparation for conflict.

Organizational Influences

Accurately understanding the difficulties described above is indispensable for defining the warning problems the IC faces; however, it is also essential to consider bureaucratic responsibilities and imperatives. The predominant factors driving the efforts of IC agencies to identify and monitor warning problems are the way departmental responsibilities are set and how priorities in support of national security objectives are established. Although all of the agencies in the IC work from the same framework of national intelligence priorities, their responsibilities often differ according to their mission areas. Historically, the IC has monitored global warning problems over the full range of regional and topical issues, but after the Cold War ended, the DCI's Task Force on Intelligence Warning noted that the IC placed an overwhelming emphasis on what was termed "big W" warning problems—major military conflict and political stability.[13] Although the IC has made adjustments in its coverage of other issues since the task force report was issued, the Department of Defense (DoD) remains concerned primarily with warning of large-scale military operations and political instability based on its planning guidance and key mission areas.[14] Although analysts within DoD monitor a wide range of enduring and emerging regional issues, the department's emphasis is centered on warning intelligence to support its highest-priority planning and crisis-response requirements. Until recently, intelligence on Russia and the former Soviet Union has had relatively low priority. As a result, the IC and DoD have devoted less analytic capacity over the past 20 years to defining Russia-related warning problems.

The final critical element in the IC's warning function has been the manner in which warning is "delivered" to policymakers and commanders. This typically has been a function of organizational and temporal factors. Because of the fluid situations that analysts monitor and report on, warning frequently occurs over a long period of time and through a wide range of IC and departmental intelligence reports. In the events examined in this report, warning

[13] DCI, 1992, p. 4.

[14] Chairman, Joint Chiefs of Staff, *Joint Intelligence*, Joint Publication 2-0, Washington, D.C., October 22, 2013, p. I-18. This publication states that "'emerging warning concerns' and 'enduring warning problems' discuss issues relevant to national security warranting DOD leadership attention." Enduring warning problems are "usually linked to contingency plans, which are defined and longstanding potential threats to US interests."

developments were reported through the *President's Daily Brief*, National Intelligence Estimates (NIEs), interagency intelligence Alert Memoranda, and Special National Intelligence Estimates (SNIEs). Individual agencies also have their own dedicated products, including the Central Intelligence Agency's (CIA's) *National Intelligence Daily* (now the *Worldwide Intelligence Review*), the Defense Intelligence Agency's *Defense Intelligence Notes*, the Chairman of the Joint Chiefs of Staff daily update briefing, and theater-specific products produced by combatant commands and the regional service components.[15] At times, these reports agree, but frequently they do not. This range of intelligence reporting mechanisms and disagreement within the community has at times led to confusion among policymakers. As an example, prior to Iraq's invasion of Kuwait, the NIO-W and his staff provided assessments that strongly disagreed with the IC's overall assessment that Iraq would not invade Kuwait.[16] In that case, competing analysis and products left policymakers to draw their own conclusions.

The type of warning delivered is also tied to the temporal aspects of any given threat and is thought of in terms of *strategic* or *tactical* warning.[17] Although these terms have been defined in earlier iterations of Director of Central Intelligence Directives (DCIDs), they have not provided a significant degree of clarity for analysts or policymakers.[18] Specifically, DCIDs on warning defined *strategic warning* as warning of war and *tactical warning* as warning of attack; however, no good definitions have been provided that allow analysts and policymakers to clearly define and understand what these concepts imply.[19] That said, the IC's role in the warning process is centered on strategic warning, with tactical warning identified as a military operational matter.[20] Strategic warning—a term originally tied to an adversary's *decision* to go to war and its subsequent *strategic preparations* to support the selected COA—is now often understood to refer to temporal conditions (i.e., early warning or notification early in a crisis), rather than to an adversary's actions. This has led many policymakers and IC managers to associate effective response with receiving warning early in the development of a crisis.[21] Clearly, early warning is generally more desirable than late warning; however, as historical examples demonstrate, adversary decisionmakers often do not make their decisions until relatively late in a crisis.

---

[15] These products are both historical and current. There have been recent changes in specific product names, but the point of this list is that multiple products from several producers offer warning-related intelligence updates.

[16] See Allen, 1998, pp. 36–38, for an excellent example of a case in which key IC elements did not agree in their assessments and reporting.

[17] Interviews conducted for recent RAND studies on warning also highlighted cases in which some DoD analysts referred to "operational" warning. This report does not address this category because it is not defined or explained in historical or current IC or DoD policy, directives, or doctrine. The interviews highlight the fact that the term is generally used in an inconsistent and imprecise manner.

[18] See DCI, 1979.

[19] Grabo, 2002, pp. 3–4.

[20] DCI, 1979; Grabo, 2002, pp. 3–4.

[21] George and Holl, 1997, p. 5.

Scenarios and Indicators: Are We Right?

Some efforts to improve warning have focused on bureaucratic and organizational changes, most of which have not led to the anticipated improvements in the IC's ability to warn.[22] Other efforts have focused on improving the IC's ability to imagine compelling and creative scenarios that might break away from the groupthink that often results from long-term focus on specific problems.[23] Analysts examining problems over a long period of time tend to develop perspectives that frequently fail to account for changes in the adversary's objectives, capabilities, and perceived security needs. Analyses of Russian operations since 2008 have attempted to identify new indicators that might improve the ability to identify Russia's preparations for hostilities at early stages.[24] Although this approach has its merits—better indicators would certainly be helpful and could lead to improved models—it could also lead to disjointed efforts focused on "boutique" or novel solutions at the expense of basic, yet still critical, research into how Russian leaders prepare for and make decisions about war. Russia's military modernization efforts since 2008 have led to significant improvements in many areas and highlight a wide variety of operational scenarios ranging from indirect action to rapid, conventional military deployments and operations.[25] Significant improvements have been made in the overall readiness, mobility, and command and control of Russia's military since 2008. There are commonalities across these areas, but there have also been important divergences in objectives, force types, and operational patterns. The countries targeted in Russia's operations raise questions about the extent to which Russian political and military leaders must prepare for outside intervention and prolonged conflict. Recent cases suggest that Russian leaders may have assessed that their actions would not precipitate either intervention or prolonged conflict; however, scenarios involving NATO allies are likely to present a different calculus.

---

[22] Betts, 1982, pp. 16, 286–287; Kam, 1988, p. 221.

[23] Recent studies that have highlighted these problems include National Commission on Terrorist Attacks Upon the United States, *The 9/11 Commission Report: Final Report of the National Commission on Terrorist Attacks Upon the United States*, New York: W. W. Norton & Company, 2004; Bob Graham, Jim Talent, and Graham T. Allison, *World at Risk: The Report of the Commission on the Prevention of WMD Proliferation and Terrorism*, New York: Vintage Books, 2008; Commission to Assess the Ballistic Missile Threat to the United States, *Report of the Commission to Assess the Ballistic Missile Threat to the United States*, Washington, D.C., July 15, 1998; *Recommendations of the Jeremiah Report*, Washington, D.C.: National Security Archive, George Washington University, MORI Doc. ID 406297, June 2, 1998.

[24] Studies dealing with war mobilization include Gustav Gressel, *Russia's Quiet Military Revolution, and What It Means for Europe*, European Council on Foreign Relations, 2016; Giles, 2016; Andrew Monaghan, *Russian State Mobilization: Moving the Country on to a War Footing*, London: Chatham House, May 2016; Julian Cooper, *If War Comes Tomorrow: How Russia Prepares for Possible Armed Aggression*, London: Royal United Services Institute, Whitehall Report 4-16, August 2016.

[25] See Gressel, 2016; Keir Giles, *Russia's "New Tools" for Confronting the West: Continuity and Innovation in Moscow's Exercise of Power,* London: Chatham House, The Royal Institute of International Affairs, March 21, 2016.

From this standpoint, the IC faces several challenges in its efforts to develop new and effective indicators for potential Russian actions, particularly in its posture toward NATO's eastern flank. A key issue will revolve around whether the IC has the capacity to perform the required detailed research over a sustained period of time.[26] The sorts of detailed indicator sets used to monitor Soviet military activities in the Cold War are probably beyond the IC's current ability to develop and monitor, due to competing collection and analytic priorities.

NIE 4-1-84, *Warning of War in Europe*, is an excellent example of an earlier, detailed indicator set in which multiple assessed COAs for a Soviet attack into Western Europe were laid out.[27] These COAs were informed by a body of intelligence detailing Soviet planning concepts, force posture, and doctrinal concepts guiding force employment. The COAs addressed in NIE 4-1-84 included (1) an attack from a peacetime posture, (2) an attack with two fronts, (3) an attack with three fronts, and (4) an attack with five fronts.[28] Each COA contained an IC assessment of the rationale and logic that likely would underpin the choice of it, the required preparations, and likely warning times given the extent of required preparation and the IC's capability to monitor these activities.

In addition, the NIE discussed a broad range of military, political, and economic preparations that would accompany each potential COA. A key point raised was the impact that war preparations would have on the civilian domain. The NIE pointed out that the preparations would occur early, and the reporting on them would be incremental, leading to increased ambiguity and varying interpretations of the meaning these indicators might have for warning of war.[29] Later, the report examined the Warsaw Pact National Defense Readiness Plan (or System) and outlined the general characteristics of peacetime-to-wartime transition processes, including national defense readiness, mobilization, economic conversion to wartime posture, and civil defense preparations.[30] The NIE also addressed (1) increased national defense readiness, (2) threat-of-war national defense readiness, and (3) full national defense readiness and the corresponding activities that were performed in each case.[31]

The NIE provided an overview of how the Warsaw Pact would go to war. It discussed not only the general perceptions among Soviet leaders about the likely paths to war, but also the range of civil and military preparations necessary for the Soviet Union and its allies to transition to a wartime footing. The primary areas it addressed were the Soviet decisionmaking process,

---

[26] Dickey, Lake, and Shachtman, 2014; Shane Harris, "Washington's Civil War over Russia Intel," *Daily Beast*, October 12, 2015; "Congress Probing U.S. Spy Agencies' Possible Lapses on Russia," 2015; Mehta, 2015.

[27] DCI, 1989.

[28] DCI, 1989, pp. 11–16.

[29] DCI, 1989, p. 20.

[30] DCI, 1989, p. 33.

[31] DCI, 1989, p. 33.

Warsaw Pact consultations, and the psychological preparation of the Soviet population.[32] The report also detailed the economic, civil defense, and military preparations that would need to be undertaken prior to war.[33]

This NIE demonstrates the level of detail the IC was able to develop on specific indicators for potential Soviet military operations. It reflected a level of effort in both collection and analysis that went well beyond general statements of military capabilities and the Warsaw Pact and Soviet military dispositions, and it also provided a robust discussion of those mechanisms that Soviet leaders viewed as essential for transitioning their population to a wartime footing. The scope of the COAs in the NIE was much broader than the scope of recent hypothesized future Russian operations; coupled with an analysis of how the Soviets would go to war, the COAs considered provided a means by which IC analysts and decisionmakers could understand more clearly the indicators they monitored. Although Russia and its military are not the same entities as those of the Soviet Union, the IC's requirement for expertise, experience, and in-depth research has not diminished. This is particularly true for analytic topics central to warning, such as logistics, mobilization, and command and control.

Another key factor in determining whether the IC is currently focused on the right scenarios and associated indicators is the rapidly changing nature of the threat. The earlier, detailed work was focused on major military operations. The IC's ability to warn was tested several times in the course of the Cold War, as the Soviets invaded Hungary, Czechoslovakia, and Afghanistan. Furthermore, many of the lessons learned from IC efforts to understand how the Soviet military operated led to improved understanding of other militaries and how other nations prepare for war.[34] Today's warning challenges associated with Russia's renewed assertiveness are more diverse and are unlikely to permit a similar sustained, in-depth focus on major military operations. One notable divergence is the speed with which Russian military reforms have occurred and the implications of these changes for the IC's ability to warn; it must be noted, however, that the qualitative impact and novelty these changes present are at times overstated. As some analysts have argued, many areas essential to Russia's recent operations—e.g., indirect warfare, mobilization, and reflexive control—were also prominent emphasis areas for the Soviet military.[35]

---

[32] DCI, 1989, pp. 34–35.

[33] DCI, 1989, pp. 36–38.

[34] Allen, 1998, pp. 33–44.

[35] Sources that describe the continuity between Soviet and Russian thinking in several areas include Timothy L. Thomas, "Russia's Reflexive Control Theory and the Military," *Journal of Slavic Military Studies*, Vol. 17, 2004, pp. 237–256; James Q. Roberts, *Maskirovka 2.0: Hybrid Threat, Hybrid Response*, MacDill Air Force Base, Fla.: Joint Special Operations University Center for Special Operations Studies and Research, Occasional Papers, December 2015; Maria Snegovaya, *Putin's Information War in Ukraine: Soviet Origins of Russia's Hybrid Warfare*, Washington, D.C.: Institute for the Study of War, Russia Report I, September 2015; Giles, 2016.

Despite the Soviet Union's collapse and the military reforms that have been under way since 2010, earlier analyses on warning of Soviet attack demonstrate that there is a wide range of factors that Russian leaders may consider in a future conflict. This is particularly true of any operation that might involve direct conflict with NATO. Although the Soviet communist party, the Soviet state, and the Soviet military no longer exist, many of Russia's senior political and military leaders were shaped by those institutions and may carry deeply held perceptions about the types of threats for which they need to plan. Recent use of indirect-action methods in Georgia and Ukraine highlight a certain level of conceptual, if not practical, continuity. Likewise, in considering new approaches to warning, IC analysts should consider the requirements that Russian political and military leaders will need to undertake in a wide range of potential scenarios. Russia's recent military operations have all been below NATO's response threshold. As such, Russian leaders could forgo certain categories of preparation that they likely would consider more carefully in a conflict with greater escalation potential, particularly one involving NATO.

Conveyance of Warning

Although it is generally understood by policymakers and commanders, a significant point must be underscored: *conveyance of warning does not connote clarity*. Ambiguity in many situations will persist even after an official warning is delivered. Furthermore, there is currently no single IC warning product. Sources of warning could be many reporting channels, including briefings, individual-agency analytic products, IC-coordinated products, and personal interactions. An additional complication could arise when disagreements within the IC lead to contradictory or competing analyses. Similarly, there may be competing assessments and understanding within or emanating from the policy community as well. Ambiguity and competing interests are likely to complicate warning in many situations.

The most significant consequence of the lack of unity in IC warning is that the IC does not have a product that delivers "unambiguous" warning to decisionmakers. Strategic warning, if provided at all, will likely be ambiguous, largely because nonmilitary indicators frequently are unclear, and many adversaries—including Russia—attempt to maintain this level of ambiguity through deception, operational security, and denial of information. As a result, decisionmakers are forced to reach conclusions based on incomplete and often unclear information. This dynamic has a significant impact on how we understand the limits of what warning can provide and the recommendations we might make to improve the IC's ability to warn.

3. Warning of Soviet Union and Russian Events

This chapter provides an overview of key themes from six major warning events involving the Soviet Union or Russia during the past 50 years. The events are not summarized or analyzed individually; rather, the focus is on themes that help identify areas where the IC has had success and areas where it has been challenged. The chapter does not present a scorecard of the community's work, nor does the discussion highlight instances in which decisionmakers did not heed warnings from the IC. Each of the events entailed some challenges that either limited or delayed the IC's ability to warn. Several also raised questions regarding decisionmakers' ability and readiness to respond to crisis events. This report considers the intelligence and policy issues together to show the symbiotic relationship that underpins the warning-response dynamic.[1] The intelligence issues involved in each event are described, and contributing factors relevant to how the IC monitored and assessed the events are outlined thematically.[2]

Bias is a core concern in the development of analysts' assessments. It is also a key element in the decision process of policymakers and commanders. Within the IC, analytic bias has long been recognized as a factor contributing to failures that occur and as a result has received considerable attention from the IC's leading analysts.[3] The themes addressed in this study are all connected to the issue of analytic bias. They include (1) Soviet or Russian activities designed to condition the expectations of outside observers, (2) the use of denial and deception to mask preparations and intent, (3) the degree to which the IC was able to attain information on Soviet or Russian activities as these crises progressed and the availability of indicators, (4) IC understanding of Soviet or Russian leadership intent, and (5) the use of indirect action as a tool to sow confusion and delay Western responses.

---

[1] These elements are discussed in greater detail in Chapter 4.

[2] The IC organization is intentionally not addressed in this study. Past efforts to reform the IC's warning capability have involved reorganization and shuffling of IC responsibilities. While in many respects these changes made sense, later studies have demonstrated that they improved the IC's warning capability only marginally, if at all. In particular, this report does not discuss recent changes in the IC's warning structure that removed the NIO-W and dispersed warning responsibility across the IC, primarily because many current and former senior IC managers (including former NIO-Ws, their deputies, and members of the National Warning Staff) believe that these changes have not necessarily led to better or worse warning capabilities. These officials believe that changes can be successful as long as the IC maintains an appropriate level of emphasis and training on warning issues.

[3] Kam, 1988, p. 214. Also see Heuer, 1999, p. 5; Rob Johnston, *Analytic Culture in the U.S. Intelligence Community: An Ethnographic Study*, Washington, D.C.: Central Intelligence Agency, Center for the Study of Intelligence, 2013, p. 10; Randall H. Pherson, "The Tradecraft of Warning: Overcoming Cognitive Barriers," paper prepared for Seminar on the Tradecraft of Warning: New Approaches and New Thinking, hosted by the ODNI's National Intelligence Council and the State Department's Bureau of Intelligence and Research, February 20, 2009, p. 1.

Themes from Warning Events

Conditioning, denial and deception, and indirect action all contribute in some way to reinforcing analysts' biases and perceptions of reality. Betts argues that "failures may not be due just to cognitive rigidity but to the ambiguity present in any disconfirming data."[4] These three factors all focus on increasing the ambiguity for analysts and decisionmakers, partly to create confusion but also to slow decisionmaking and responses as observers attempt to make sense of a situation. Furthermore, they at times present information that may confirm expectations or deny information that signals preparations and intent.

Indicators and leadership intent are also areas in which analytic bias can influence the IC's ability to warn. In the absence of data regarding an adversary's doctrine, objectives, operational concepts, and training patterns, analysts are forced to rely on their own templates, which are most likely shaped by U.S. concepts. Indicators based on these concepts may embed biases in analysts' minds in ways that are difficult to overcome. In particular, as new evidence regarding an adversary's actual methods for operating becomes available, information that disconfirms earlier assessments will often have to meet a higher standard to change perceptions and estimates.[5] Similarly, expectations of how foreign leaders will react in a given situation are often based on analysts' expectations of rational and reasonable behavior rather than on a thorough understanding of perceptions shaping those leaders' decisions.[6]

The IC exerts considerable effort to combat analytic bias. For example, Intelligence Community Directive (ICD) 203 is designed to improve the quality of IC analysis. Objectivity is the first of nine analytic tradecraft standards designed to prevent analysts from being "unduly constrained by previous judgments when new developments indicate a modification is necessary."[7] The ICD highlights the need for "reasoning techniques and practical mechanisms that reveal and mitigate bias."[8] Analytic training programs, product evaluations, and the use of structured analytic techniques are all tools currently in use within the IC to address this persistent concern.[9] The themes discussed in this chapter all likely contributed to or reinforced analytic biases in historical and recent warning events.

---

[4] Betts, 1982, p. 123.

[5] Betts, 1982, p. 123. See also Grabo, 2002, p. 53. Grabo points out that indicators, to the greatest extent possible, should be based on an adversary's doctrine, practice, and plan. When information in these areas is not available, analysts must rely on other practical or theoretical considerations for developing indicators.

[6] Graham Allison and Philip Zelikow, *Essence of Decision: Explaining the Cuban Missile Crisis*, New York: Longman, 1999, pp. 80–81.

[7] Director of National Intelligence, 2015, p. 2.

[8] Director of National Intelligence, 2015, p. 2.

[9] An overview of IC use of structured analytic techniques today is presented in Artner, Girven, and Bruce, 2016.

Denial and deception played a conditioning role in some of the events and is closely linked to indirect action in some instances. For this study, events have been placed in the most relevant categories, but with the understanding that some may demonstrate multiple attributes.

The events chosen to examine how the U.S. IC warned against the Soviet Union or Russia are (1) the Cuban missile crisis, (2) the Soviet invasion of Czechoslovakia, (3) the Soviet invasion of Afghanistan, (4) Russia's invasion of Georgia, (5) Russia's invasion of Crimea and operations in eastern Ukraine, and (6) Russia's deployment to Syria. The central themes in these events were also present in a wider body of warning failures that did not involve Soviet or Russian operations. Additional examples are provided to help illustrate practices that have proven effective in achieving surprise.[10] These examples all have commonalities that shape our recommendations for improving warning.

Conditioning

A key element contributing to surprise in several historical examples was conditioning, or the habituation of key activities or deployments to create in the target's mind a new sense of normalcy.[11] Conditioning activities are effective in reducing the diagnostic value of key indicators and limiting reaction time. They have factored heavily in Soviet and Russian operations since the Soviet invasion of Czechoslovakia in August 1968. Four of the events considered in this chapter—the Soviet invasions of Czechoslovakia and Afghanistan and the Russian incursions into Georgia and Ukraine/Crimea—involved some type of activity that likely constitutes conditioning.

Prior to its invasion of Czechoslovakia, the Soviet Union announced a series of Warsaw Pact exercises that would take place in Czechoslovakia and Poland in June 1968. This exercise, named Sumava, provided cover for the introduction and maintenance of Warsaw Pact forces in Czechoslovakia. Although the exercise was supposed to have ended on June 30, Soviet news agency TASS retracted its announcement that the exercise had ended to provide cover for continued troop presence.[12] Subsequently, the Soviets announced a rear-services exercise covering an area from Latvia to Ukraine. The exercise involved recalling reservists,

---

[10] Additional examples include North Korea's invasion of South Korea in 1950, China's intervention in the Korean War in 1950, the Suez Crisis of 1956, the Six-Day War in 1967, the Yom Kippur War in 1973, and Iraq's invasion of Kuwait in 1991. See Allen, 1998, pp. 33–44; Abraham Ben-Zvi, "The Study of Surprise Attacks," *British Journal of International Studies*, Vol. 5, No. 2, July 1, 1979, pp. 129–149; Betts, 1982; Michael I. Handel, "The Yom Kippur War and the Inevitability of Surprise," *International Studies Quarterly*, Vol. 21, No. 3, September 1, 1977, pp. 461–502; Kam, 1988; Barton Whaley, *Stratagem: Deception and Surprise in War*, Norwood, Mass.: Artech House, 2007.

[11] Betts, 1982, p. 66. One prominent example is the Israeli Air Force (IAF) training activity prior to its attack on Egyptian airfields at the outset of the Six-Day War in 1967. The IAF had modified its training patterns as early as two years prior to the initial strike. This modification established a baseline of normal activity for the Egyptian military that removed what would have been a critical indicator.

[12] Cynthia M. Grabo, "Soviet Deception in the Czechoslovak Crisis," *Studies in Intelligence*, Vol. 14, No. 1, Spring 1970, pp. 19–34.

requisitioning civilian transportation assets, and bringing decommissioned military equipment back on line.[13] Additional exercise activity involved a command post and communications exercise involving Soviet, East German, Czech, and Polish forces inside Czechoslovakia that ran from late July until August 10 and an air-defense exercise that ended on August 20.[14] The relatively lengthy period of exercise activity led the majority of the IC's analysts to conclude that these were, in fact, exercises and not a mobilization and deployment of forces for invasion.[15] Further, the buildup, under the guise of maneuvers, led to a "cry wolf" effect that was accentuated by routine press leaks from Western governments.[16]

Similarly, the IC concluded that Soviet force deployments and activities prior to entering Afghanistan in December 1979 were exercises or shows of force rather than preparations for an invasion.[17]

Recent Russian operations in Georgia and Ukraine have continued the practice of exercises serving as both signals and cover activities for military operations. In 2008, Russian forces conducted exercise Kavkaz 2008 in the North Caucasus Military District, which ran from mid-July until August 4. The numbers of forces involved in the exercise were underreported in the Russian press to dispense with any obligations to invite foreign observers.[18] In addition, a sizable number of forces did not depart once the exercise had concluded, and they eventually were used during the invasion on August 8.[19]

Prior to Russia's invasion and annexation of Crimea in March 2014, several exercises took place involving multiple branches of Russia's military. Many of the exercises were surprise inspections designed to test readiness. The sixth exercise began on February 26 and involved 150,000 servicemen, 90 aircraft, 120 helicopters, 880 tanks, 1,200 other pieces of equipment, and 80 ships.[20] As this surprise inspection commenced, the Russian Ministry of Defense issued

---

[13] Grabo, 1970.

[14] CIA, *The CIA and Strategic Warning: The 1968 Soviet-Led Invasion of Czechoslovakia*, Washington, D.C.: undated, pp. 9–10; Whaley, 2007, pp. 522–523; Grabo, 1970, pp. 29–30.

[15] Grabo, 1970, p. 30.

[16] Whaley, 2007, p. 521.

[17] Douglas MacEachin, *Predicting the Soviet Invasion of Afghanistan: The Intelligence Community's Record*, Washington, D.C.: Center for the Study of Intelligence, 1999, p. 22. Also see DCI, Interagency Intelligence Memorandum 80-10017JX, *The Soviet Invasion of Afghanistan*, October 1980, pp. 17–18.

[18] C. W. Blandy, *Provocation, Deception, Entrapment: The Russo-Georgian Five Day War*, Shrivenham, UK: Advanced Research and Assessment Group, Defence Academy of the United Kingdom, March 2009, p. 5.

[19] Andrei Illarionov, "The Russian Leadership's Preparation for War, 1999–2008," in Svante E. Cornell and S. Frederick Starr, eds., *The Guns of August 2008*, Armonk, N.Y.: M. E. Sharpe, 2009, p. 73.

[20] Johan Norberg, *Training to Fight: Russia's Major Military Exercises 2011–2014*, Swedish Defense Research Agency, November 2015, pp. 49–50. Norberg cites the following sources for these numbers: Ministry of Defense of the Russian Federation, "Voiska (sily), zadeistvovannye v proverke boevoi gotovnosti perebrasivaiutsia v aznachennye raiony," February 27, 2014, and Ministry of Defense of the Russian Federation. "Severny i Baltiiski floty v ramkakh vnezapnoi proverki boevoi gotovnosti narashivaiut sostav sil v akvatoriiakh Barentseva i Baltiiski morei," February 27, 2014.

16 reports about it, each reiterating the number and types of forces involved.[21] These reports also included the distances from which the forces were deployed, to emphasize their "endurance, persistence, and durability."[22] As events developed, senior IC officials were accused of not providing adequate warning, but they countered that they had regularly provided decisionmakers with updates and potential Russian COAs.[23]

These examples illustrate how "routine" military deployments or exercise activity can be used as a means to cover operational intent and preparations. Successful use of such activities can reduce an adversary's sensitivity to certain indicators. While most such exercises are nothing more than routine events, if performed over an extended period of time, they may reduce the intended target's sensitivities and decrease the diagnostic importance of key indicators. Furthermore, these events may lead intelligence organizations to "cry wolf"—potentially desensitizing intelligence analysts and policymakers alike. Although there is a risk of overstating this effect, the more routine an activity becomes, the less it serves as a marker capable of signifying change from peacetime norms to potential threat.[24]

Conditioning may also include the deployment of additional forces to a region in ways that are wholly consistent with Russia's threat perceptions but not necessarily indicative of an impending attack. For instance, deployments of additional or supplementary air and air-defense units may reflect a heightened concern that is not connected to plans to conduct offensive operations in a designated time frame. Likewise, the addition of new ground units to the Western Military District cannot automatically be interpreted as a short-term indicator or an act of conditioning.[25] Nevertheless, these types of action can condition analysts' sensitivity and reduce the diagnostic value of key indicators.

Denial and Deception

Denial and deception is closely linked with conditioning, but it encompasses a much wider range of activities. Denial includes "activities and programs designed to eliminate, impair, degrade or neutralize the effectiveness of intelligence collection," while deception refers to the "manipulation of intelligence collection, analysis, or public opinion . . . with the intent of

---

[21] Norberg, 2015, p. 50.

[22] Norberg, 2015, p. 50.

[23] Jeremy Herb, "Clapper: Ukraine Was Not an Intelligence Failure," *The Hill*, March 10, 2014.

[24] McCreary, 1983, p. 76. McCreary argues that the "cry wolf" syndrome should not be confused with near misses, which he asserts "are mixes of accurate and inaccurate judgements, which are better termed as near misses and remote misses." McCreary believes that both of these outcomes should be considered successes because they frequently lead to heightened sensitivity.

[25] Thomas Grove, "Russia Says It Is Creating Three New Divisions to Counter NATO Moves," *Wall Street Journal*, May 4, 2016.

manipulating perceptions of policy makers in order to influence their actions and decisions."[26] The impact of denial and deception is hard to overstate. It has played a significant role in many historical intelligence failures,[27] including several warning events involving the Soviet Union or Russia. As in the case of conditioning, official media reporting often has obscured the actual scale of activities involved (e.g., Kavkaz in 2008), provided false information on exercise dates (e.g., Sumava in 1968), or provided cover for operational activities outside the scope of an exercise (e.g., Georgia and Ukraine).

Many of Russia's current denial and deception capabilities consist of such traditional *maskirovka* (deception) activities as camouflage, subversion, sabotage, propaganda, and psychological operations.[28] Recent denial and deception efforts have included the use of unmarked military equipment, cyber operations, passportization,[29] clandestine infiltration of military personnel, and media manipulation. These actions may not be sufficient to comprehensively mask Russian operations, so they are generally used to delay reactions within the target state and the international community. Deception is not necessarily meant to mask all preparatory or early activities. Rather, its primary purpose is to provide an initial, insurmountable advantage by creating doubt sufficient to slow down an adversary's reaction time. The activities do not need to be flawless or sophisticated. They need only to be good enough to create confusion.

Denial and deception activities were present in all six of the events studied here. Prior to the invasion of Czechoslovakia in 1968, Warsaw Pact exercises were used as a cover for force movements that would later be used for the invasion itself. Analysts reported these exercises in a variety of NATO and U.S. intelligence publications.[30] In its attempt to mislead the United States and NATO, the Soviet media reported that these exercises were nothing more than routine exercises that occurred every year at the same time.[31] This deception was relatively simple, and later examples included similar actions. The use of exercises to mask military movements played a role in Russian incursions in both Crimea and Georgia. Furthermore, the use of special-forces

---

[26] Roger Z. George and James B. Bruce, *Analyzing Intelligence: Origins, Obstacles, and Innovations*, 2d ed., Washington, D.C.: Georgetown University Press, 2008, p. 280.

[27] George and Bruce (2008, pp. 193–204) examined eight historical intelligence failures: Pearl Harbor, the Cuban missile crisis, the Yom Kippur War, the Iranian Revolution, India's nuclear test, the Soviet biological weapons program, 9/11, and Iraq's weapons-of-mass-destruction (WMD) program. They found that in five of the eight cases (Pearl Harbor, the Cuban missile crisis, the Yom Kippur War, Soviet biological weapons, and Iraq's WMD), deception was a factor, and that denial was a factor in all cases.

[28] Roberts, 2015, p. 1.

[29] Passportization is a Russian program that gives Russian passports to foreign citizens, primarily in former Soviet territories. It has been used extensively in Abkhazia, South Ossetia, Crimea, and eastern Ukraine.

[30] Euan G. Davis and Cynthia M. Grabo, "Strategic Warning and Deception," *Studies in Intelligence*, Vol. 17, Spring 1973, p. 38; Whaley, 2007, p. 521.

[31] Davis and Grabo, 1973, p. 38.

troops in foreign uniforms (i.e., in Afghanistan) or uniforms with no insignia (i.e., in Crimea) succeeded in creating confusion and delaying responses from the targeted governments.

In the Cuban missile crisis, denial and deception efforts to hide the nature of hardware deliveries were buttressed by Soviet Premier Nikita Khrushchev's assurances that missiles would not be deployed to Cuba. Although this deception eventually was uncovered, in other operations, it was effective in creating doubt and delaying reactions as operations unfolded. A particular challenge that must be considered when evaluating the IC's warning capabilities against Russia is the extent to which U.S. and NATO collection and analytic capabilities will be able to identify deception, particularly in situations where Russian units are already forward-located and indirect warfare operations are under way. Currently, IC analysts receive limited, if any, training in countering denial and deception, and education and training opportunities to improve these capabilities are few.[32]

In Georgia and Crimea, Russian forces—both regular and special—also attempted to conceal their status by wearing uniforms without insignias.[33] These activities were not designed to prevent detection and provide plausible deniability indefinitely, nor were they elaborate. Russia intended them to create confusion in the target countries and among potential Western responders. The U.S. and European responses were subsequently slowed as both governments and publics grappled with the events that were unfolding.

Available Information and Indicators

In each of the six events, the IC tracked numerous key indicators or events. The community was aware of abnormal levels of activity, and the activities seemed to be responding to international tensions at the time they were initiated. In each case, the information about potentially troubling Soviet or Russian activities was abundant. As discussed earlier, the IC had spent considerable time developing indicator lists for different scenarios during the Cold War. During the Cuban missile crisis, the IC concluded that the Soviet deliveries to Cuba were intended to "substantially improve air defense and coastal defense capabilities in Cuba" because the Soviets hoped to enhance Castro's defensive capabilities and deter future attempts to overthrow his regime.[34] IC analysts were able to detect the transfer of a dozen SA-2 SAM systems and their subsequent deployment to fixed sites, a dozen MIG-21s, tanks, self-propelled artillery, and Komar-class patrol boats.[35] The IC's ability to detect specific systems at the time demonstrates that the community was well aware of the military-equipment deliveries, with more

---

[32] This conclusion was drawn from interviews with current and former IC managers conducted during other RAND projects.

[33] Snegovaya, 2015, pp. 11–12.

[34] Office of National Estimates, *The Military Buildup in Cuba*, Special National Intelligence Estimate 85-3-62, September 19, 1962, p. 2.

[35] Office of National Estimates, 1962, p. 5.

likely to follow. But the ability to monitor these shipments and determine the types of systems being delivered provided little insight into Soviet leadership intentions regarding Cuba. In this case, the IC's close monitoring of conventional systems presented ample information to support an alternative, reasonable conclusion that the Soviet shipments were designed to build up Cuba's defenses.

The same largely held true for the later Soviet invasions of Czechoslovakia and Afghanistan. IC analysts were able to effectively monitor the types of forces being moved, general categories of activity, and other preparations, including mobilization efforts and logistics preparations. As in the instances of conditioning, the IC monitored military indicators based on the major exercises under way at the time.[36] The IC also closely followed nonmilitary indicators, such as official Soviet press reports and leadership meetings and movements. It monitored the pace and frequency of key Politburo meetings held to discuss the situation in Czechoslovakia and observed the departure from Moscow and subsequent return of Politburo members in early and mid-August 1968.[37]

In the lead-up to the Soviet invasion of Afghanistan, IC analysts were able to observe and monitor several similar indicators. As early as August 1979, analysts began to see activity within key units just north of the Soviet border with Afghanistan. This activity included a Guards Airborne Division engaged in specialized loading techniques with advanced military transport aircraft.[38] The IC was also able to identify a wide range of activity that included the presence of military advisers, involved logistics, and revealed support operations that seemed to suggest either large-scale signaling or preparations for military operations. As events in Afghanistan continued to spiral out of control, there were several indicators that involved the introduction of Soviet special forces units and high-level political deliberations. Although it was aware of all these indicators, which correlated with the IC's indicator list at the time, the IC remained uncertain about the Soviet Union's actual role in Afghanistan's internal political power struggles and whether its leaders were contemplating potential military options or simply signaling.[39] This suggests that even when the IC has well-developed indicators and the capability to monitor them, the indicators can lead analysts to plausible, but inaccurate, explanations regarding the nature of the activities being monitored.

The IC also had no shortage of pre-conflict indicators of more-recent Russian operations in Georgia, Ukraine, and Syria. Despite the diminished priority of gathering intelligence on Russia—a fact reflected in the IC's overall level of collection and analysis devoted to the Russian problem—there was a wide-scale awareness of Russian military activity during each

---

[36] Grabo, 2000, pp. 522–523.

[37] CIA, undated, pp. 14–15.

[38] MacEachin, 1999, p. 22.

[39] MacEachin, 1999, pp. 24–27.

period.[40] In short, the IC possessed considerable information about Russian military movements in the recent Russian aggression in Georgia, Ukraine, and Syria. The primary problem that inhibited both U.S. and NATO responses was described by former CIA Director Michael Hayden, who commented, "This is less a question of how many collection resources we throw at Russia and more broadly about the analytic challenge of understanding Putin's mind set."[41] As these three events reveal, quality indicators that reflect the IC's best knowledge of how an adversary makes decisions and operates are important. Absent these indicators, the United States and its allies would have little basis for anticipating potential conflicts and hot spots; however, even when numerous indicators are present, they are often not sufficient to reveal Soviet or Russian intentions in time to prevent surprise or enable timely policy responses.

Leadership Intent

In many respects, the IC is capable of identifying anomalous activities through collection and analysis. The indicators in the events studied here clearly make this point. The IC's primary challenge in many of these situations was understanding the motivations and intentions of Soviet or Russian decisionmakers. Commenting on the IC's assessment of Soviet ballistic missile emplacements in Cuba, Sherman Kent noted, "No estimating process can be expected to divine exactly when the enemy is about to make a dramatically wrong decision . . . we could not believe that Khrushchev could make such a mistake."[42] In several other situations, IC analysts and policymakers also did not conclude that Soviet or Russian activities were necessarily pretexts for military operations, largely because they had limited or conflicting information on leadership intent. As a result, they argued that Soviet or Russian interests would not be advanced by the aggressive courses of action the leaders eventually chose.

The most significant challenge for analysts remains adversary intentions, primarily because "intentions are sometimes different from what state decisionmakers will actually do."[43] Furthermore, most policymakers may not be able to fully predict an adversary's emotional responses to situations in which its goals and values are changed by evolving developments. These situations highlight the difficulties Kent and the IC faced during the Cuban missile crisis—often, the logic of risk versus reward is not what analysts anticipate and is guided by a wider range of perceptions and internal drivers that are difficult to grasp.

Another dynamic that complicates the problem of understanding adversary intentions is the role played by the leaders of U.S. partner nations. In the invasions of Czechoslovakia,

---

[40] Dickey, Lake, and Shachtman, 2014; "Congress Probing U.S. Spy Agencies' Possible Lapses on Russia," 2015; "US Intelligence Lapse on Russian 'Surprise' Moves in Syria Probed," *Newsmax*, October 8, 2015; Harris, 2015.

[41] Dickey, Lake, and Shachtman, 2014.

[42] Michael Douglas Smith, "The Perils of Analysis: Revisiting Sherman Kent's Defense of SNIE 85-3-62," *Studies in Intelligence*, Vol. 51, No. 3, 2007, p. 4.

[43] Betts, 1982, p. 54.

Afghanistan, Georgia, and Ukraine, the political actions of U.S. foreign leaders played a significant role in Soviet and Russian decisions to invade. Understanding adversaries is thus not the only variable influencing the ability to provide timely warning. Understanding the intentions of third-party leaders is also essential and has proven to be a difficult complication. In 2008, U.S. policymakers were concerned that Georgian President Saakashvili would feel compelled to respond to Russian activities in Abkhazia because of internal Georgian politics, most notably a parliamentary election scheduled in late May. The U.S. policymakers were hearing an increasing number of discussions through diplomatic channels indicating that Georgian leaders, including Saakashvili, were coming to the conclusion that they had to respond to Russian provocations in the near term or risk losing Abkhazia.[44] These discussions were never official; however, they involved U.S. and European Union representatives and involved all levels of Georgian security officials, including the president. They reflected a sense of desperation and a perceived imperative to protect Georgian citizens.[45] Russian leaders did not miss the opportunity to use these discussions to their advantage. The Russian media broadcast reports that Georgia was planning military action, and the Russian defense chief warned that there would be a war in Georgia if steps were not taken to avoid conflict.[46]

One of the most common recommendations following a warning failure is to "improve collection."[47] This is often accompanied by efforts to create and monitor new warning indicators. In most cases, however, the "lack of information and warning indicators is usually not the reason for failure of estimates."[48] The primary analytic challenge to successful warning remains that of accurately identifying and understanding leadership intent during crisis situations. Improving IC understanding of adversary intentions is an enduring problem, particularly as it relates to warning decisionmakers of adversary objectives and planning in specific situations. Decisionmakers seeking better warning must understand the limits this long-term challenge imposes on the warning products they are likely to receive in crisis situations and the implications those limits have on their ability to respond in a timely fashion.

Indirect Action

Indirect action—e.g., intimidation, political meddling, subversion, pressure, and shows of force—featured as prominently in the earlier Soviet operations as it does today. Military forces can perform indirect actions both in peacetime, as part of nonmilitary operations such as

---

44 Ronald Asmus, *A Little War That Shook the World: Georgia, Russia, and the Future of the West*, Basingstoke, UK: Macmillan, 2010, p. 152.

45 Asmus, 2010, p. 151.

46 Asmus, 2010, p. 149.

47 Kam, 1988, p. 222.

48 Kam, 1988, p. 222.

peacekeeping, and in war.[49] Most significantly, indirect and direct warfare do not exist in an either/or relationship—they can be practiced simultaneously. Indirect action was a component in two of the three Soviet events examined in this study. The Soviet coup carried out prior to the invasion of Afghanistan consisted of Spetznaz troops being inserted into Kabul in Afghan Army uniforms. As part of the operation, they seized and cordoned off key political and military facilities as other forces attacked the presidential palace.[50] Indirect-warfare actions in Czechoslovakia and Afghanistan included the use of false media reports designed to influence or shape responses in victim countries or their allies, the use of intelligence services to foment internal dissent and co-opt corrupt leaders and security officials, and diplomatic coercion.

These operations also figured prominently in both Georgia and Ukraine. Prior to Russia's invasion of Georgia, Moscow had developed key themes that focused on painting Saakashvili as the aggressor. Moscow contended that Saakashvilli's actions forced Russian intervention to protect Russian citizens.[51] A key element in advancing this story was the deployment of 48 Russian journalists to the area the day before to the Russian operation.[52] Russia also employed advanced media operations in Ukraine and Crimea in 2014. The guiding principle of these operations was to "direct the message or narrative" by controlling language; this was the "first step to the control of meaning, and the manipulation of meaning the first step in the manipulation of politics."[53] The subsequent employment of "political technology" encompassed a full range of media and cyber operations designed to shape public perceptions, obscure facts on the ground, and present orchestrated myths to undermine the adversary government's control.[54]

Russia also relied on a wide variety of nonmilitary measures in Georgia and Ukraine as part of a broader effort to discredit its opponents and set conditions that would eventually permit Russian forces to gain control with a minimum of resistance. Cyber operations played a significant role in both countries, as did the use of Russia's intelligence services to co-opt and discredit corrupt and/or sympathetic local officials.[55] By issuing Russian passports in South Ossetia and Abkhazia, a process known as "passportization," Russian officials were able to claim that their intervention was primarily an effort to protect Russian citizens and compatriots.[56] In

---

[49] V. V. Serebryannikov, "Thoughts on the Concept of 'War,'" *Voyennaya Mysl*, October 1, 2004.

[50] MacEachin, 1999, p. 35.

[51] Paul A. Goble, "Defining Victory and Defeat: The Information War Between Russia and Georgia," in Svante E. Cornell and S. Frederick Starr, eds., *The Guns of August 2008: Russia's War in Georgia*, Armonk, N.Y.: M. E. Sharpe, 2009, p. 182.

[52] Goble, 2009, p. 186.

[53] Andrew Wilson, *Ukraine Crisis: What It Means for the West*, New Haven, Conn.: Yale University Press, 2014, p. 21.

[54] Wilson, 2014, pp. 34–36. For additional discussions of specific aspects of these operations, see Giles, 2016.

[55] Mark Galeotti, *Putin's Hydra: Inside Russia's Intelligence Services*, European Council on Foreign Relations, Policy Brief, May 2016, p. 7.

[56] Illarionov, 2009, pp. 56–57.

both Georgia and Ukraine, Russia used irregular forces and local patriotic groups to prevent the appearance of Russian involvement, create confusion among Georgian and Ukrainian security forces, and provide cover for threatening activities by disguising them as local, organic responses to the central government's policies.[57]

Indirect action was an important part of Soviet operations and remains important in Russian operations. It is highly unlikely that its importance will diminish. On the contrary, its use has proven highly effective and will probably increase in the future. This presents a key challenge for warning, because it is unclear whether these actions will provide analysts with diagnostic value as indicators, particularly in cases where they may reflect ongoing activities in other areas of interest. On the surface, it would appear that they are quality indicators; however, our best insights into how indirect activities support larger operations are derived from hindsight. Further complicating their potential value as indicators is the fact that they do not appear to conform to a predictable, doctrinal template in the same manner that many military operations do. Indirect actions, such as "passportization," cyber attacks, and influence campaigns orchestrated by Russian media and intelligence organizations, often take place over extended periods of time. Russia is conducting these types of activities today against NATO and non-NATO nations alike.[58] As such, they might serve, at best, as limited tools to help analysts understand the transition from peace to war.

The Current Russia Warning Challenge

The events in which the themes outlined above were identified are largely viewed as warning failures, though not without some level of disagreement among both policymakers and intelligence analysts. On the basis of the IC's performance in gathering intelligence on Russia since 2008—informed, in part, by statements from policymakers who are consumers of intelligence—one could conclude that there are major shortfalls in the United States' ability to warn. This is particularly relevant in the context of potential Russian operations against the Baltics. However, several key factors raise questions about whether this conclusion is merited. There are definitely shortfalls, but the shortfalls serve to illuminate several persistent problems.

Since the end of the Cold War, and particularly since the 9/11 attacks, Russia's importance as a national security priority has diminished significantly, and this has had an overall negative impact on the intelligence resources devoted to the Russian problem. The 2002 *National Security Strategy of United States* stated that "with Russia, we are building a new strategic relationship"

---

[57] Snegovaya, 2015, pp. 11–12.

[58] Julian E. Barnes, "NATO Works to Adapt to More Ambiguous Warfare Techniques," *Wall Street Journal*, February 8, 2016; "From Cold War to Hot War: Russia's Aggression in Ukraine Is Part of a Broader, and More Dangerous, Confrontation with the West," *The Economist*, February 12, 2015; Juris Kaža and David Gauthier-Villars, "Latvia's Wariness over Russia Raises Civil Rights Concerns at Home," *Wall Street Journal*, August 26, 2016.

and "the United States and Russia are no longer adversaries."[59] Later versions echoed partnership with Russia on key issues. Although the strategies expressed concerns about democratic reform and human rights, they did not speak of Russia as a security concern.[60] The National Security Strategy characterized Russia as an aggressor and security concern only in 2015, following its annexation of Crimea and intervention in eastern Ukraine.[61] By this time, the IC's focus on Russia had diminished significantly, along with the numbers of collectors and analysts devoted to monitoring it. This fact was recognized by senior government officials, including the commander of the U.S. European Command and the deputy secretary of defense.[62] Despite having limited resources, the IC was able to monitor most of the relevant Russian activities that were under way prior to hostilities. More recently, the IC has directed an increase in Russia's priority relative to other major issues such as terrorism and China.[63]

During each of the Soviet-era crises, the IC had significant collection assets and analysts devoted to monitoring the Soviet Union.[64] Although the IC has recently increased the personnel and resources targeting Russia to roughly 10 percent of its total collection and personnel resources, this still represents a marked decrease from the roughly 40 percent devoted to the Soviet Union during the Cold War.[65] The number of analysts working on Soviet/Russian issues has fallen from 13,000 at the end of the Cold War to roughly 1,000.[66] In addition, senior leaders have acknowledged a decrease in the level of expertise on Russia.[67] During the Cold War, IC analysts had significantly more information available to them across a wide number of critical topics. Large numbers of analysts could analyze their data sources to identify critical characteristics that formed the basis of the U.S. government's understanding of the Soviet threat, its decisionmaking processes, and the major processes by which the Soviet military transitioned for war. The overwhelming number of analysts and collection assets dedicated to warning of potential Soviet or communist aggression demonstrated clearly that this was the IC's top priority at that time.[68] This priority was reflected in detailed indicator lists, substantial attention to the

---

[59] The White House, *The National Security Strategy of the United States*, September 2002, p. 26.

[60] The White House. *The National Security Strategy of the United States*, March 2006, p. 38–39; The White House, *The National Security Strategy of the United States*, May 2010, pp. 11, 44.

[61] The White House, *The National Security Strategy of the United States*, February 2015, p. 25.

[62] Mehta, 2016; Burgess Everett and Josh Gerstein, "Why Didn't the U.S. Know Sooner?" *Politico*, March 5, 2014.

[63] Miller, 2016.

[64] Julian E. Barnes, "NATO's Breedlove Calls for Sharper Focus on Russia Ahead of Departure," *Wall Street Journal*, May 1, 2016.

[65] Miller, 2016.

[66] Miller, 2016.

[67] Jim Garamore, "Work Discusses Russia with Military, Intelligence Leaders," *DoD News*, *Defense Media Activity*, April 17, 2015; Miller, 2016.

[68] This priority is evident in the terms of reference documents issued for the IC Watch Committee under the DCI's auspices. These terms of reference ran through much of the 1950s and 1960s. See DCI, Directive No. 1/2, *Terms of*

Soviet Union as a warning problem, and detailed products such as the 1980 Interagency Intelligence Memorandum *The Soviet Invasion of Afghanistan: Implications for Warning* and the 1984 NIE *Warning of War in Europe*.[69] In all of the events discussed in this report involving the Soviet Union, collection and analysis were well covered. During each event, collectors and analysts with extensive experience on the Soviet target were able to monitor key political and military activities.

In several of the more-recent events involving Russia, even if the IC had reporting of the decision to invade at its earliest point, policymakers would have had limited time to formulate options, select a COA and implement it. The final Politburo decisions to invade Czechoslovakia and then Afghanistan do not appear to have been made until relatively late in the crises. After the invasion of Czechoslovakia, many IC analysts concluded that the decision to invade may have been made between two key meetings of Czech and Soviet leaders at the end of July and first week of August, approximately two or three weeks prior to the invasion.[70] Similarly, the decision to invade Afghanistan likely came in early to mid-December—only weeks prior to Soviet troops crossing the border.[71] In both cases, even if analysts had known of the plan at the exact moment the Soviet decision was made, the best-case warning scenario would have been a few weeks, and it is unclear what options would have been available to policymakers even if they had been given "unambiguous warning."

Similarly short timelines between decisions and actions have characterized events involving Russia. Senior U.S. decisionmakers were informed and concerned about Russian activities in South Ossetia and Abkhazia as early as April 2008.[72] Some information suggested that the Russian decision to invade was made at about that time. However, with Georgia's close proximity and Russia's forward force presence, any final decision to halt and reinitiate operations into those republics was on a timeline determined by Russian decisionmakers.[73] Likewise, the Russian intervention in Crimea and eastern Ukraine appears to have been decided on a relatively short timeline in response to sudden and unpredictable events in Ukraine, although planning for these operations could have been carried out well in advance. As these examples—along with Russia's Syria deployment—demonstrate, Russian decisions have followed closely on the heels of crisis events (e.g., the collapse of the Yanukovych government in Ukraine and perceived Georgian and NATO provocations). Furthermore, because of

---

Reference, Watch Committee of the IAC (11 May 1954), December 15, 1976; DCI, Directive No. 1/5, *Terms of Reference, Watch Committee of the IAC*, effective March 7, 1961; DCI, Directive No. 1/5, *Terms of Reference, Watch Committee of the IAC*, effective August 8, 1962, editorially revised February 27, 1963.

69 DCI, 1980; DCI, 1989.

70 CIA, 2010, pp. 11–12.

71 MacEachin, 1999, pp. 46–48.

72 Asmus, 2010, p. 152.

73 Asmus, 2010, pp. 168–169.

geographic proximity and RFAF forward positioning, Russia's leaders can delay a decision until the situation is more critical, even if RFAF actions are discovered.

Frequently, IC analysts are expected to warn about events before an adversary's decisionmakers have settled on a COA. As Hayden noted, it is not clear what options to prevent, deter, or dissuade Russian actions the short period of additional warning would have provided for U.S. and NATO policymakers.[74] The same could be argued for the invasions of Czechoslovakia and Afghanistan. These considerations indicate that regardless of whether or not early warning is provided, the United States and its allies must consider viable policy options prior to any event. To present an effective deterrent, the deliberations must include resource and force-posture considerations. Absent these conditions and the corresponding national security interest, early warning will not help bolster NATO's posture on its eastern flank.

The problem of understanding Russian intentions has likely become more difficult as a result of Russia's current leadership and decisionmaking processes. This is not to suggest that Soviet decisionmaking was transparent—it clearly was not. However, there was a collective Soviet leadership whose meeting and deliberations could be followed to some extent.[75] In contrast, today's Russian leadership decisionmaking cycle is centered on Vladimir Putin and a very small circle of advisers. Their intentions are notoriously difficult to understand, primarily because they are contextual and can change on relatively short notice to adjust to new conditions or information.[76] In this situation, the IC often is forced to rely on processes and activities that provide only indirect reflections of intent.

The IC's ability to warn is clearly stressed. Demands have grown, and less expertise is now devoted to the countries that make up the former Soviet Union, including Russia. Over the past 15 years, priority and resources devoted to Russia generally fell behind those devoted to Afghanistan, Iraq, global terrorism, China, and the Middle East. Now, Russia has emerged as a national security priority and its military planners in multiple commands, crisis support in Ukraine and Syria, and a host of current and long-term policy issues are placing ever-greater demands on the IC's Russia analysts. As Grabo argues in her seminal work on warning, research is the key to warning. In today's environment, the requirement for intelligence to meet immediate needs is likely to inhibit the IC's ability to perform the in-depth research necessary to improve warning. This is particularly the case in situations that might involve escalation, especially with NATO, but only indirect insights into leadership intent are available.

The themes of Russian aggression and the IC's current capabilities identified in this report are not new. With more emphasis now being placed on Russia, the IC's ability to warn would probably be improved by rebuilding the IC's bench of experts and in-depth knowledge of Russia.

---

[74] Dickey, Lake, and Shachtman, 2014.

[75] This factor was noted in both the Czechoslovakia and Afghanistan examples discussed earlier.

[76] McCarthy, 1994, p. 7.

The examples presented here should help set boundaries for what decisionmakers realistically can expect in terms of warning; however, they also highlight the need to ensure that warning remains an actual priority rather than a stated priority. Faced with demands for current intelligence, the IC often finds it expedient to sacrifice long-term research to meet immediate needs. In this context, intelligence analysis is not a "free" commodity. Devoting analytic capacity to one subject generally means that capacity cannot be used for another subject, and many areas in which warning has proven important in the past still require expertise and sustained attention.

4. The Warning-Response Dynamic and NATO's Eastern Flank

Although "early warning is a prerequisite both for any prudent decision to act and for effective action itself," many factors contribute to leaders' tendency to delay hard decisions as long as possible.[1] The reasons for the delays vary widely and may include perceived high risks of possible actions, the desire for more clarity in an uncertain situation, and reluctance to modify or discard policies as warning intelligence becomes available.[2] Even in situations where policymakers receive early and convincing warning, they must weigh decisions and potential responses against competing priorities shaped by U.S. national interests and available resources. Events involving the Soviet Union and Russia have clearly presented questions about whether realistic courses of action were available even had unambiguous warnings been received earlier in the crises.

In the context of the current U.S. force posture in Europe and the state of NATO's readiness, the question of whether or not the IC can provide adequate warning will remain a dominant issue. Since the last major U.S. Army units in Europe left in 2012, there has been an increasing concern with the problem of confronting potential Russian aggression in the Baltics. Recent NATO actions following the Wales and Warsaw summits indicate movement in a direction that demonstrates NATO's increased resolve to confront the Russian threat there; however, if Russia decided to mount a major operation in the Baltics, U.S. and NATO decisionmakers would have only limited ready options. Recent war games and analysis have highlighted this challenge. In several scenarios, Russian forces are able to achieve their objectives within 60 hours. Even with significant advanced warning and acceptance by decisionmakers, the United States and its allies would have only a limited capacity to put military options into motion.[3] Other studies have highlighted the threat posed by Russian anti-access/area-denial capabilities against U.S. and NATO efforts to deter and, if needed, respond to Russian military actions.[4] These capabilities present significant challenges to U.S. and allied regional force projection, particularly as they relate to the early employment of NATO airpower. In addition, they complicate the ability to bring forces from outside of Europe to reinforce the limited numbers currently forward-positioned there. The ambiguity in early warning may slow the decision to deploy the NATO Response Forces, including the Very High Readiness Joint Task Force, when there is

---

[1] George and Holl, 1997, p. v.

[2] George and Holl, 1997, pp. 4–5; Robert Jervis, "Why Intelligence and Policymakers Clash," *Political Science Quarterly*, Vol. 125, No. 2, June 2010, pp. 196–198.

[3] Shlapak and Johnson, 2016, p. 8.

[4] Kathleen H. Hicks, Heather Conley, Lisa Sawyer Samp, Jeffrey Rathke, Olga Oliker, and Anthony Bell, *Evaluating Future U.S. Army Force Posture in Europe: Phase I Report*, Center for Strategic and International Studies, February 2016, p. 2.

disagreement within the alliance on the nature of the crisis.[5] It may take from days to weeks for follow-on forces to arrive, depending on the speed with which NATO decisionmakers can decide on a COA, the readiness posture of these forces, and the speed with which Russian forces can achieve their objectives.[6]

Statements by senior officials in the U.S. government, including then-President Obama, verify that Russia has once again become a matter of national priority and highlight the importance of warning about activities on NATO's eastern flank.[7] NATO leaders have also announced posture changes that include the deployment of four battalions intended to deter Russian aggression.[8] Political resolve, particularly among NATO allies, and future deployments may enhance NATO's ability and willingness to respond; nevertheless, several factors make warning on NATO's eastern flank a particular challenge. Even in the most favorable circumstances, these factors make the warning-response dynamic in the area particularly problematic.

The region's geography and the RFAF's physical proximity, juxtaposed with NATO's very thin posture in the area today, present a significant challenge for warning. Because of their forward location and significant numbers, the Russians do not need to deploy large forces forward to pose a threat to the Baltic states. This situation denies the IC a number of military indicators. Furthermore, Russia's forward forces possess significant advantages in mobility, firepower, and air defenses. Even with NATO's upcoming posture enhancement, Russian forces have an overwhelming advantage. Preparations to bring in additional RFAF units to defend against NATO follow-on attacks likely could be undertaken either after initial operations were under way or relatively late in the pre-conflict preparations. While there may be an increase in indirect action prior to a major conventional operation, such indicators will remain largely ambiguous and difficult to distinguish from similar activities currently under way in a number of countries along Russia's periphery.

In 2013, the RFAF reintroduced no-notice inspections, or "snap" exercises, that have since been carried out on both a territorial and a functional basis.[9] These events present several difficulties for warning and have generated concern among NATO's senior political and military leaders.[10] One immediate concern is that these activities may be intended to condition U.S.

---

[5] Hicks et al., 2016, p. 10.

[6] Shlapak and Johnson, 2016, pp. 8–10, Hicks et al., 2016, pp. 10–11.

[7] "Press Conference by President Obama After NATO Summit," The White House, Office of the Press Secretary, July 9, 2016.

[8] Julian E. Barnes and Thomas Grove, "NATO Set to Approve Baltic Force at Warsaw Summit," *Wall Street Journal*, July 7, 2016.

[9] Norberg, 2015, p. 24.

[10] "Press Conference by NATO Secretary General Jens Stoltenberg Following the Meeting of the NATO-Ukraine Commission at the Level of Defence Ministers," North Atlantic Treaty Organization, June 15, 2016; Michael R.

analysts and policymakers into viewing them as the routine, normal course of Russian military activity. In several historical and recent Soviet and Russian examples, exercises have been used to mask military preparations, divert attention, and create confusion.[11] The earlier Soviet exercises involved multiple types of forces, logistics, and mobilization preparations. Since reinstituting the snap exercises in 2013, Russia has performed at least 18 of them nationwide.[12] Furthermore, there have been multiple inspections and exercises involving the Western Military District in various capacities.[13] During one period that began with Russia's invasion of Crimea and ended with its deployment to Syria—February 2014 through September 2015—Russia carried out six no-notice inspections.[14]

Russia's revitalized strategic exercise program also presents several warning concerns, particularly large-scale military operations that may require wider mobilization and integration of nonmilitary governmental organizations. Annual strategic exercises run by the Ministry of Defense involve all organizations concerned with Russia's military security. Past exercises have included the Interior Ministry and the Federal Security Service.[15] These exercises regularly involve participation from all services and multiple military districts across the RFAF. Furthermore, they are designed to improve Russia's capabilities for transitioning from peacetime to wartime. The exercises also involve more-complex scenarios involving senior political decisionmakers and military leaders.[16] Overall, Russia's annual strategic exercises are a concrete reflection of the military reform efforts initiated following its 2008 miscues in Georgia. Along with the now-routine no-notice inspections, these exercises demonstrate Russia's will to upgrade the readiness of its armed forces and prepare them for a wide range of future military operations.

The final factor significantly complicating the warning-response dynamic is the regularity with which Russia has either used force or threatened its use in recent years. Such activities, along with the regularity of large-scale military exercises, leave policymakers and analysts pondering what's next. In this context, understanding intentions becomes especially problematic for providing warning. U.S. and NATO policymakers and the IC do not understand well the potential triggers for action and the decisionmaking process that determines how and where Russia's forces will be committed. Because of the opacity of this process, additional insight and knowledge of Russian decisionmaking will come slowly, at best. Moreover, Russian decisions

---

Gordon, "NATO Commander Says He Sees Potent Threat From Russia," *New York Times*, April 2, 2014; Andrew Tilghman, "EUCOM Commander: US May Need to 'Puncture' Russian-Defenses," *DefenseNews*. March 1, 2016.

[11] Adrian Croft, "NATO Commander Plays Down Tension with Russia over Ukraine," *World News*, February 27, 2014.

[12] Hicks et al., 2016, pp. 2–3.

[13] Lukasz Kulesa, "Towards a New Equilibrium: Minimising the Risks of NATO and Russia's New Military Postures," European Leadership Network, Policy Brief, February 8, 2016, pp. 42–44.

[14] Kulesa, 2016, pp. 42–44.

[15] Norberg, 2015. p. 12.

[16] Norberg, 2015, p. 23.

and subsequent preparations can be tailored to counter U.S. and NATO responses. This possibility presents the classical warning dilemma: When warning is successful, the adversary modifies its behavior.[17] If behavioral modifications become known, the event is considered a success; however, they frequently go undetected. In these situations, both policymakers and analysts run the risk of falling prey to the "cry wolf" syndrome, becoming desensitized, or falsely reading adversary intentions.

Potential Areas for Improving Warning

Although warning certainly can be improved, there are no guarantees for success. Some areas for improvement involve IC practices, while others rely on policymaker and commander decisions among the competing priorities that confront IC collectors and analysts. Furthermore, waiting for additional confirmation of Russian intentions may leave little time for policy responses that require building domestic political consensus, generating coalition acceptance, or deploying additional forces.

Generally, the IC's most effective warning will likely be based on its own assessments of Russian leadership intent or indirect reflections of intent, both of which are often ambiguous. The following discussion presents recommendations for improving warning against Russia on NATO's eastern flank.

Rebuild Capacity to Obtain Intelligence About Russia's Targets

Recent changes in the nature of the threat from Russia have made it necessary to rebuild the government's expertise on Russia and to gain additional capacity in areas relevant to warning.[18] Current challenges stem, in part, from shifts in both collection and analytic resources as new priorities have emerged over the past 25 years. Assets that during the Cold War would have been focused on monitoring key political and military trends in Russia have been devoted to other priority areas. The numbers of Russia analysts in the IC has fallen substantially, along with the overall level of expertise and experience. Although the IC is unlikely to need the same numbers of analysts it needed during Cold War, sustained attention will be needed to identify emerging Russian military operational concepts and norms as well as order-of-battle changes. Simultaneously, with Russian forces engaged in eastern Ukraine and Syria, IC analysts must devote significant time to crisis support and monitoring, at the expense of research in areas necessary for enhancing warning. These requirements, coupled with the growing challenge of monitoring and analyzing Russian information operations and indirect-action activities in other parts of Europe, suggest that the IC may need additional capacity to maintain awareness of Russian operations over a wide geographic area.

---

[17] McCreary, 1983, pp. 74–75.

[18] John Grady, "EUCOM Emphasis Shifting to Russian Deterrence," *USNI News*, July 14, 2016; U.S. European Command, *U.S. European Command Posture Statement 2016*, February 25, 2016; Garamore, 2015.

In the absence of additional capacity to support its expanding list of tasks, the IC's ability to provide policymakers and commanders with penetrating insight will potentially remain constrained. The shortage of analysts with expertise in areas relevant to key warning issues may slow the IC's efforts to improve warning as new analysts are brought up to speed. These delays, in turn, may limit the IC's ability to provide timely warning of Russian actions that negatively impact U.S. and NATO security. This is particularly true with IC managers being asked to balance increasing requirements for current intelligence (including crisis support) and the need for sustained research efforts that may pull analysts away from immediate needs.

Since analysts appear to have monitored Russian movements and disposition in recent events relatively successfully, despite the difficulty the IC has traditionally experienced with understanding adversary intentions, some might conclude that additional capacity is not needed. This argument ignores the significant transformation Russia's military is now pursuing. Frequent and more-complex exercises are specifically designed to improve RFAF readiness and shorten response times. Mobilization and nonmilitary crisis preparations are also designed to effectively and quickly transition Russia to a war footing. These factors, coupled with an opaque decisionmaking structure and a much more aggressive posture, emphasize the need for innovative strategies to improve warning in an increasingly complex environment.

Finding new ways to gain insight into Russian intentions (either directly or indirectly) will require long-term, sustained research and in-depth analysis. This effort should include rebuilding expertise on historical precedents, legal and regulatory structures, organizational changes, procedural modifications, experimentation, and other military and nonmilitary activities that support Russian wartime transition efforts.

Improved Indicators

The understanding of warning must not devolve simply into a discussion of indicators. Warning entails much more than that, although well-developed sets of indicators can contribute enormously to warning success. Rigorously and systematically building indicator lists helps analysts think through the conceptual models that lie beneath their analysis of how Russia might pursue specific types of operations. The examples cited in this study demonstrate that building quality indicators requires that the IC be capable of collecting and monitoring them on a regular basis, that they are diagnostic for the warning problem they support, and that the IC has the requisite expertise to understand the nuances and differences that indicate changes from steady-state to crisis situations.

Strategies for collecting new indicators will require detailed analysis of activity patterns, technical parameters, and systemic relationships. RFAF modernization efforts and the pace of change in Russia's military make these analyses an increasing challenge. Furthermore, tailored collection focused on key events, such as exercises or operational experiments, requires an understanding of objectives and tasking. Nevertheless, the ability to understand systemic relationships will permit collectors to identify other means of tracking key indicators and potentially counter denial and deception efforts.

Another key element of the indicator-development process is ensuring that indicators have diagnostic value and are related to some critical function in the peace-to-war transition. Russia's use of no-notice inspections since 2013, along with a heavy forward presence along NATO's eastern flank, has probably made many of the military indicators that would be useful for early warning less important than they once were. This is particularly true as Russia builds readiness in top-echelon units. Even though widespread military preparations will remain necessary large-scale operations, they will require much less time in the future and will probably present a less observable footprint. Furthermore, many out-of-area preparations, such as deployment of air, airborne, and air-defense units, could be undertaken shortly before early operations begin. In fact, a rapid-deployment capability has been a key feature of recent exercises. Russia conducted 11 no-notice inspections in the first half of 2014 that included inspections of up to 65,000 servicemen and deployments that averaged up to 350 km to reach exercise areas.[19] The largest no-notice inspection occurred immediately before Russia's invasion of Crimea and included 150,000 servicemen and significant numbers of tanks, heavy equipment, aircraft, and ships.[20]

While the value of some military indicators may be diminished, other areas may emerge as new possibilities. One of the key functions of annual exercises and no-notice inspections is war preparation. Detailed collection and analysis in both categories of activities could illuminate preparatory functions that must take place at the operational and strategic levels of war. In addition, because the exercises are an important element in training military staffs and political leaders, there may be key procedures and practices that can be identified and monitored. Understanding these processes and any criteria or measures of effectiveness used for evaluating readiness could provide critical nontactical indicators.

In addition to understanding the military dimensions of the Russian exercises, it is necessary to understand important crisis-management elements involving nonmilitary entities. Though these elements may not be useful for developing indicators for small operations (that presumably would not involve foreign intervention or escalation), they may have significant diagnostic value for operations potentially involving action by U.S. or NATO forces. Nonmilitary exercises could indicate essential wartime functions that are focused on ensuring internal stability and supporting key mobilization processes. In addition, they also may provide information on important civil-defense and disaster-preparedness functions.

A final set of indicators worth exploring are those tied to mobilization. Russian laws define mobilization as the process by which the Russian Federation transitions from a peacetime to a wartime posture by ensuring access to necessary logistics and infrastructure and ensuring the

[19] Norberg, 2015, p. 51.

[20] Norberg, 2015, p. 58.

security of the civilian population.[21] It must be emphasized that mobilization in this context is not limited to military mobilization. Military mobilization is an essential function—and one that entails a plethora of critical functions to manage civil-military relations—but it is not the only element of mobilization. The IC's earlier warning paradigm was focused heavily on monitoring military mobilization. This overreliance led to significant problems and, according to one former NIO-W, contributed to several warning failures.[22] Subsequent research demonstrated that many authoritarian regimes and centrally planned economies "prepare for war by first initiating measures across the spectrum of social, economic, political, and military life that divert resources away from civilian life and into the armed forces."[23] Accordingly, the potential social and economic disruptions caused by war preparations are likely to weigh heavily on foreign decisionmakers' thinking about maintaining social stability. Understanding these nonmilitary indicators will require a wide range of expertise, but they provide improved insight into adversary intent.

Although collection and analysis of these indicators is feasible, the issues involved are less relevant to many intelligence consumers on a day-to-day basis. With limited resources, IC managers will have to consider the relative importance of perceived current intelligence requirements (particularly those not tied directly to decisions or those that simply build situational awareness) as opposed to warning.

Focused Training

In recent years, the IC has developed many analytic training courses that are available to analysts at all agencies. These resources are essential for maintaining a professional and proficient analytic corps. However, two key areas of training, both tied closely to warning, have been cut back greatly. The first is warning training itself. When the Director of National Intelligence decided to disestablish the category of NIO-W in late 2010, the prevailing logic was that warning is a responsibility of all IC managers and analysts. Numerous current and former IC senior analysts and managers did not see this thinking as inherently problematic for warning, as long as analysts were properly trained, so warning training has been reduced significantly.[24] Currently, the vast majority of IC analysts receive only a limited introduction to warning in their core analytic training.[25]

---

[21] An example of these laws is Federal Law No. 31-FZ of February 26, 1997, *On Mobilizational Preparations for the Mobilization of the Russian Federation*, February 26, 1997 (with the amendments and additions of July 16, 1998, March 24, December 30, 2001).

[22] Allen, 1998, p. 1.

[23] Allen, 1998, p. 3.

[24] This conclusion is derived from interviews conducted during recent RAND studies on strategic warning.

[25] This conclusion is derived from interviews conducted during recent RAND studies on strategic warning.

Another potential shortfall is in denial and deception training. As noted earlier, a significant number of warning failures have resulted from successful denial and/or deception efforts by an adversary. Denial and deception played at least some role in each of the six events examined in this study. Nevertheless, the IC provides very little training on how to counter adversary denial and deception, and relatively few IC analysts are trained in this area, particularly as it relates to the practice of warning.[26] Denial and deception has been a key part of Soviet and Russian thinking. By failing to address this fundamental area, the IC is likely to face additional challenges to its already stressed warning capabilities.

Build and Leverage Experience and Expertise

Because the number of experienced IC analysts dedicated to studying Russia has declined greatly since the end of the Cold War,[27] this group faces many of the same challenges as other parts of the IC in terms of experience and expertise. To improve warning, the IC should build both experience and expertise in its Russia collection and analytic workforce. Although this will not be a quick fix, it will be necessary to address this complex problem.

More Directed Research

The recommendations outlined here cannot be accomplished without more focus on directed research. To be useful for supporting improvements in warning, research should be focused on immediate issues that will illuminate key problems that Russian political and military leaders believe they will have to address in a crisis or wartime situation. Research on longer time horizons is unlikely to be useful for warning to most, if not all, policymakers, because of their immediate policy and security concerns.

Directed research must be focused on identifying new sources of information and new approaches to understanding Russian planning and decisionmaking. Similarly, the IC should devote additional resources to in-depth collection and analysis focused on critical processes in a range of activities, including mobilization, disaster/crisis response and preparedness, and civil defense. Improvements in this area would be helpful in identifying the types of social, political, and economic processes that are critical for transitioning from peace to war.

Warning and Decisionmaking

The primary focus of this study is the IC's current warning capability and areas in which it might be improved. An additional theme that emerged from the events examined is the warning-response dynamic, particularly as it relates to perceptions about what warning will be able to

[26] George and Bruce, 2008, pp. 211–212, 344. These themes were raised by senior IC managers and analysts during interviews conducted for other projects on strategic warning.

[27] Miller, 2016.

deliver in the available decision space and time. It is unclear whether additional warning time would have allowed policymakers to develop better, more-effective policy options in many of the events. There was an imbalance in the level of interest and importance that each side (Soviet Union/Russia and the United States/NATO) assigned to the situations being monitored. As a consequence, the Soviets and Russians were much more willing to take action than the United States and NATO were to respond to it. In this sense, the policy options were limited.

In some examples, the question of force posture was also an issue. The United States and NATO would have had to significantly increase force posture prior to responding in several of these instances, so the Soviet or Russian action would have been well under way (possibly completed) and considerably more difficult to address. Recent analyses and war games have highlighted a similar situation on NATO's eastern flank, where Russian forces are forward-deployed and overmatch their NATO adversaries. Russian decisionmakers are also in a position to make decisions that are best suited to a given situation. If their actions are discovered, they have the ability to pull back and wait for another day. If conditions are favorable, Russian forces could rapidly achieve their objectives, well before NATO could respond in a meaningful manner. Even under the best conditions, improved warning will not improve this reality on the ground. Additionally, it is unlikely that earlier warning—which is typically more ambiguous—would do little to convince allied decisionmakers who are reluctant to take action in the first place. It may, in fact, complicate allied buy-in because of its ambiguity.

Warning is essential to the time policymakers have to make decisions and the quality of those decisions. Less time and poor-quality information are likely to have a direct, negative impact on crisis decisions. Areas where policymakers can help sharpen the IC's focus, clarify what they want from intelligence, and define their priorities and concerns are described briefly below.

Outline Priorities

Policymakers can help improve warning by clarifying priorities and providing insight into their policy initiatives and concerns. Warning on NATO's eastern flank will remain a high priority, but in the midst of other concerns about Russia's next moves, this priority may lag as policymakers demand more information on other problems. Although the IC cannot dedicate its resources to only a limited number of issues—it must monitor a much wider range of activities—analytic resources that might otherwise be focused on covering lower-priority issues should be devoted to identifying processes, functions, and new indicators for identifying systemic change.

In general, circumstances requiring rapid responses that may involve deploying military forces—including an attack in the Baltics—should have highest warning priority. Other responses that are more likely to lead to punitive measures, such as sanctions or support to opposition groups, may not require the same level of early warning. In fact, they may require a lengthy period for formulating and then gaining approval of a specific policy choice.

Realistic Expectations

If policy options are limited from the outset, there is little that advanced warning can do to mitigate the effects of an adversary's actions. To get the kind of warning they want from the IC, policymakers must make sure they have realistic expectations about what the IC is capable of providing. As emphasized throughout this study, understanding adversary intent has been a constant challenge for the IC. The IC has been taken to task for not providing early warning in several situations in which the final Soviet or Russian COA was probably not decided until very late in the crisis. This problem was most significant where geographic proximity and force posture permitted the Soviets to make a late decision (i.e., in the Soviet invasions of Czechoslovakia and Afghanistan and the Russian invasion of Crimea). A similar situation now confronts the IC and policymakers with respect to NATO's eastern flank. The RFAF's proximity and already significant force posture provide Russia with a range of options that will permit its decisionmakers to employ forces on relatively short notice or when opportunities present themselves.

When IC analysts have information available that allows them to provide early warning, the information is frequently ambiguous and even contradictory. This is particularly the case when military indicators are not the primary evidence. Issues tied to Russian decisionmaking are generally fragmentary and reflect the IC's limited understanding of adversary decisionmaking. Indicators tied to mobilization and other nonmilitary preparations could also explain a range of activities other than large-scale military activity. Russian indirect action is a primary example. Indirect activities are ongoing in several areas today. In Georgia, they were under way for years prior to the onset of the operation, and they continued after it concluded. However, detecting and attributing these activities is also a major challenge. Warning based on indicators of these types of action will generally have a high level of ambiguity, and waiting for improved certainty will increase risk for U.S. and NATO policymakers in many situations.

Realistic Options

The final element of the warning-response dynamic is ensuring that realistic options are considered and available prior to an event. In several of the examples discussed in this study, the range of potential responses was limited, for a variety of reasons. Earlier warning in these situations may have done little to provide more options. As a result, it is imperative that for high-priority interests that involve significant threat, policymakers must consider the available options ahead of time and plan accordingly.

5. Conclusions

Russian forces have conducted three major military operations over the past nine years and are in the midst of a major modernization effort. Accordingly, the demand for intelligence on Russia continues to grow, while policymakers and analysts discuss a wide range of potential scenarios for the future. These scenarios range from Russian meddling in the affairs of former Soviet states with limited Western ties to major operations against former Soviet states that are now NATO members.[1] The pace at which the IC is being forced to work in this region is unparalleled since the end of the Cold War. Russia's emergence as a national security priority presents a host of new challenges to meet multiple planning and policy requirements throughout the U.S. government.

Achieving timely warning has proven extremely difficult, for a variety of reasons, in large part because of a lack of insight into Russian leadership intentions. This shortfall is compounded by Russia's geographic proximity to many of the areas where its forces have been committed or may be committed in the future. Other factors, such as denial and deception, have also played a significant role in preventing effective warning. With other high-priority issues competing for policymaker attention and intelligence resources, the current warning posture vis-à-vis Russia arguably could be the most challenging problem facing the IC today.

The themes discussed in this report involve several cross-cutting issues that have challenged the IC, regardless of resources or experience. These themes suggest that persistent problems, including Russian leadership intent, place limits on what the IC will be able to warn about on a consistent basis. The themes also demonstrate that while developing and monitoring indicators are important parts of the warning process, they have not always led to success, and they provide no guarantee of improved warning in the future. In each of the events discussed in this study, the IC was aware of indicator-based activities just prior to hostilities. When it came down to a final assessment, however, the IC misjudged or lacked insight into Soviet or Russian willingness to undertake the courses of action the leaders chose. In each instance, the IC's judgments were reasonable. In Afghanistan, archival records from Soviet Politburo meetings showed that some members argued against an invasion and raised many of the same points the IC used in concluding that the Soviets would not invade. In the end, these arguments did not prevail, and Soviet forces invaded.

---

[1] The variety of reporting on future scenarios involving Russia is discussed in many studies, including Stephen Blank, "Why Does Putin Surprise Us Again and Again?" Atlantic Council, March 7, 2016; "Determining Putin's Next Target," *Stratfor*, February 22, 2016; Bridget Kendall, "What Next for President Putin?" *BBC News*, December 31, 2015; Luke Coffey, "Predicting Putin's Next Move," *Al Jazeera*, November 30, 2015; Marvin Kalb, "Putin's Deceptive Pause: What Are Russia's Next Steps in Ukraine?" Brookings Institution, September 1, 2015; Steven L. Hall, "Why the West Should Pay More Attention to Moldova," *Stratfor*, February 20, 2016.

Despite the recurring challenges, warning can be improved. The recommendations presented in Chapter 4 are an important start. By developing the IC's expertise and analytic capacity, IC analysts and collectors could more effectively tackle the toughest intelligence needs associated with warning. Improved analytic capacity and information would enable the type of in-depth research that is currently so challenging for the IC because of its current personnel shortages and increasing workload. Achieving the needed improvements will not be a short-term endeavor. Success requires time and sustained focus, even when demands for current intelligence routinely emerge. With limited IC resources currently dedicated to Russia, most collection and analysis will focus on issues demanding immediate attention. This translates into a day-to-day emphasis on producing current intelligence at the expense of the types of in-depth research necessary for improved warning. Senior-leader statements and the need to deal with Russia's reprioritization indicate that more people and capabilities likely will become available. DoD's emerging strategic initiative on Russia is designed, in part, to help rebuild expertise in the IC and the department.[2] Over the near to mid-term, other programs may introduce additional projects that will support decisionmakers' warning needs.

Rededication of Cold War–level resources to the Russia problem is unlikely, particularly in light of the multitude of competing priorities. It also is not necessary, with today's advanced collection technologies and information systems and tools supporting analysts. While Russia's recent actions may threaten U.S. and NATO interests, they do not constitute the same level of threat the Soviet Union posed, from a variety of perspectives. Nevertheless, analytic effort should be dedicated to research to improve the IC's current indicators, develop better understanding of key civil-military processes and functions necessary for transitioning to war, and rebuild the experience and expertise on Russia the IC has lost over the past two decades. Clearly, these changes would not in themselves solve all the warning problems. They could, however, put an already stressed IC in a position where its prospects for successfully warning policymakers and commanders will improve with time.

Improved warning will do little without an enhanced U.S. and NATO forward presence. This is particularly true regarding NATO's eastern flank. Russian forces possess significant advantages, and the time between a Russian decision and the beginning of operations could be short—as little as two weeks or less. With Russia's efforts to improve the speed with which it can mobilize and deploy its forces, these timelines are likely to become even shorter in the future. In areas where there is an already overwhelming Russian advantage, increased warning time will be highly unlikely, and marginal warning improvements will offer little value to policymakers and commanders. Bolstering U.S. and NATO posture will remain the best option for deterring future Russian aggression in the Baltics.

---

[2] John Grady, "EUCOM Emphasis Shifting to Russian Deterrence," *USNI News*, July 14, 2016; U.S. European Command, 2016.

References

Ackoff, Russell, "Towards a System of System Concepts," *Management Science*, Vol. 17, No. 11, July 1971. As of August 13, 2017: http://ackoffcenter.blogs.com/ackoff_center_weblog/files/ackoffsystemofsystems.pdf

Allen, Charles E., "Warning and Iraq's Invasion of Kuwait: A Retrospective Look," *Defense Intelligence Journal*, Vol. 7, No. 2, 1998.

Allison, Graham, and Philip Zelikow, *Essence of Decision: Explaining the Cuban Missile Crisis*, New York: Longman, 1999.

Argyris, C., *Knowledge for Action: A Guide to Overcoming Barriers to Operational Change*, San Francisco: Jossey-Bass, 1993.

Artner, Stephen, Rich Girven, and James Bruce, *Assessing the Value of Structured Analytic Techniques in the U.S. Intelligence Community*, Santa Monica, Calif.: RAND Corporation, RR-1408-OSD, 2016. As of August 13, 2017: https://www.rand.org/pubs/research_reports/RR1408.html

Asmus, Ronald, *A Little War That Shook the World: Georgia, Russia, and the Future of the West*, Basingstoke, UK: Macmillan, 2010.

Barnes, Julian E., "NATO's Breedlove Calls for Sharper Focus on Russia Ahead of Departure," *Wall Street Journal*, May 1, 2016. As of August 14, 2017: http://www.wsj.com/articles/natos-breedlove-calls-for-sharper-focus-on-russia-ahead-of-departure-1462115561

———, "NATO Works to Adapt to More Ambiguous Warfare Techniques," *Wall Street Journal*, February 8, 2016. As of August 14, 2017: http://www.wsj.com/articles/nato-works-to-adapt-to-more-ambiguous-warfare-techniques-1454928411

Barnes, Julian E., and Thomas Grove, "NATO Set to Approve Baltic Force at Warsaw Summit," *Wall Street Journal*, July 7, 2016. As of August 14, 2017: http://www.wsj.com/articles/nato-set-to-approve-baltic-force-at-warsaw-summit-1467894778

Ben-Zvi, Abraham, "The Study of Surprise Attacks," *British Journal of International Studies,* Vol. 5, No. 2, July 1, 1979.

Betts, Richard K., "Analysis, War, and Decision: Why Intelligence Failures Are Inevitable," *World Politics*, Vol. 31, No. 1, October 1978.

———, *Surprise Attack: Lessons for Defense Planning*, Washington, D.C.: Brookings Institution Press, 1982.

———, "Surprise Despite Warning: Why Sudden Attacks Succeed," *Political Science Quarterly*, Vol. 95, No. 4, December 1980.

Blandy, C. W., *Provocation, Deception, Entrapment: The Russo-Georgian Five Day War*, Advanced Research and Assessment Group, Shrivenham, UK: Defence Academy of the United Kingdom, March 2009. As of August 14, 2017: https://www.files.ethz.ch/isn/97421/09_january_georgia_russia.pdf

Blank, Stephen, "Why Does Putin Surprise Us Again and Again?" Atlantic Council, March 7, 2016. As of March 14, 2017: http://www.atlanticcouncil.org/blogs/ukrainealert/why-does-putin-surprise-us-again-and-again

Central Intelligence Agency, *The CIA and Strategic Warning: The 1968 Soviet-Led Invasion of Czechoslovakia*, Washington, D.C., undated. As of August 14, 2017: https://www.cia.gov/library/readingroom/docs/2009-09-01.pdf

———, *Strategic Warning & the Role of Intelligence: Lessons Learned from the 1968 Soviet Invasion of Czechoslovakia*, Washington, D.C.: Center for the Study of Intelligence, 2010. As of August 13, 2017: https://www.cia.gov/library/publications/cold-war/czech-invasion/soviet%20-czech-invasion.pdf

Chairman, Joint Chiefs of Staff, *Joint Intelligence*, Joint Publication 2-0, Washington, D.C., October 22, 2013.
As of August 13, 2017:
http://www.dtic.mil/doctrine/new_pubs/jp2_0.pdf

Coffey, Luke, "Predicting Putin's Next Move," *Al Jazeera*, November 30, 2015. As of August 14, 2017: http://www.aljazeera.com/indepth/opinion/2015/11/predicting-putin-move-151130110004214.html

Commission to Assess the Ballistic Missile Threat to the United States, *Report of the Commission to Assess the Ballistic Missile Threat to the United States*, Washington, D.C., July 15, 1998.

Cooper, Julian, *If War Comes Tomorrow: How Russia Prepares for Possible Armed Aggression*, London: Royal United Services Institute, Whitehall Report 4-16, August 2016.

Croft, Adrian, "NATO Commander Plays Down Tension with Russia over Ukraine," *World News*, February 27, 2014. As of August 14, 2017: http://www.reuters.com/article/us-ukraine-crisis-breedlove-idUSBREA1Q1F220140227

Davis, Euan G., and Cynthia M. Grabo, "Strategic Warning and Deception," *Studies in Intelligence*, Vol. 17, Spring 1973.

"Determining Putin's Next Target," *Stratfor*, February 22, 2016. As of August 14, 2017: https://www.stratfor.com/image/determining-putins-next-target

Dickey, Eli, Noah Lake, and Christopher Shachtman, "Ex-CIA Chief: Why We Keep Getting Putin Wrong," *Daily Beast*, March 2, 2014. As of August 12, 2017: http://www.thedailybeast.com/articles/2014/03/02/ex-cia-chief-why-we-get-putin-wrong.html

———, "U.S. Spies Said No Russian Invasion of Ukraine—Putin Disagreed," *Daily Beast*, March 1, 2014. As of August 12, 2017: http://www.thedailybeast.com/articles/2014/02/28/u-s-spies-said-no-invasion-putin-disagreed.html

Director of Central Intelligence, *DCI Task Force Report: Improving Intelligence Warning*, May 29, 1992, approved for public release April 25, 2012.

———, Directive No. 1/2, *Terms of Reference, Watch Committee of the IAC (11 May 1954)*, December 15, 1976.

———, Directive No. 1/5, *National Intelligence Warning,* May 23, 1979 (document superseded DCID No. 1/5, effective May 18, 1976).

———, Directive No. 1/5, *Terms of Reference, Watch Committee of the IAC*, effective March 7, 1961.

———, Directive No. 1/5, *Terms of Reference, Watch Committee of the IAC*, effective August 8, 1962, editorially revised February 27, 1963.

———, Interagency Intelligence Memorandum 80-10017JX, *The Soviet Invasion of Afghanistan*, October 1980. As of August 14, 2017: https://www.cia.gov/library/readingroom/docs/DOC_0000278538.pdf

———, *Warning of War in Europe: Changing Warsaw Pact Planning and Forces*, Memorandum to Holders, NIE 4-1-84, September 1989. As of August 13, 2017: ttps://www.cia.gov/library/readingroom/docs/DOC_0000265626.pdf

Director of National Intelligence, *Analytic Standards*, ICD 203, January 2, 2015. As of August 14, 2017: https://www.dni.gov/files/documents/ICD/ICD%20203%20Analytic%20Standards.pdf

Entous, Adam, Julian E. Barnes, and Siobhan Gorman, "Without Warning: U.S. Scurries to Shore Up Spying on Russia," *Wall Street Journal,* March 24, 2014. As of August 12, 2017: https://www.wsj.com/articles/u-s-scurries-to-shore-up-spying-on-russia-1395625416

"EUCOM Commander: US May Need to Puncture Russian Defenses," *DefenseNews*, March 1, 2016. As of August 15, 2017: https://www.defensenews.com/global/europe/2016/03/01/eucom-commander-us-may-need-to-puncture-russian-defenses/

Everett, Burgess, and Josh Gerstein, "Why Didn't the U.S. Know Sooner?" *Politico*, March 4, 2014. As of August 14, 2017: http://www.politico.com/story/2014/03/united-states-barack-obama-ukraine-crimea-russia-vladimir-putin-104264.html

"Exclusive: Congress Probing U.S. Spy Agencies' Possible Lapses on Russia," Reuters, October 8, 2015. As of August 12, 2017: http://www.reuters.com/article/us-mideast-crisis-intelligence-exclusive/exclusive-congress-probing-u-s-spy-agencies-possible-lapses-on-russia-idUSKCN0S20CZ20151008

Federal Law No. 31-FZ, *On Mobilizational Preparations for the Mobilization of the Russian Federation*, February 26, 1997 (with the amendments and additions of July 16, 1998, March 24, December 30, 2001).

Freedberg, Sydney J., Jr., "Europe Needs Intel, Ships, & Focus: Gen. Breedlove," *Breaking Defense*, October 30, 2015. As of August 10, 2017: http://breakingdefense.com/2015/10/europe-needs-intel-ships-high-level-focus-gen-breedlove/

"From Cold War to Hot War: Russia's Aggression in Ukraine Is Part of a Broader, and More Dangerous, Confrontation with the West," *The Economist*, February 12, 2015. As of August 14, 2017: http://www.economist.com/news/briefing/21643220-russias-aggression-ukraine-part-broader-and-more-dangerous-confrontation

Galeotti, Mark, *Putin's Hydra: Inside Russia's Intelligence Services*, European Council on Foreign Relations, Policy Brief, May 11, 2016. As of August 12, 2017: http://www.ecfr.eu/publications/summary/putins_hydra_inside_russias_intelligence_services

Garamore, Jim, "Work Discusses Russia with Military, Intelligence Leaders," *DoD News, Defense Media Activity*, April 17, 2015. As of August 10, 2017: https://www.defense.gov/News/Article/Article/604483/work-discusses-russia-with-military-intelligence-leaders/

George, Alexander L., and Jane E. Holl, *The Warning-Response Problem and Missed Opportunities in Preventive Diplomacy*, New York: Carnegie Commission on Preventing

Deadly Conflict, Carnegie Corporation of New York, May 1997. As of August 13, 2017: https://www.carnegie.org/media/filer_public/33/6e/336e40fd-5176-42c2-bb9d-afd7b3b6550a/ccny_report_1997_warning.pdf

George, Roger Z., and James B. Bruce, *Analyzing Intelligence: Origins, Obstacles, and Innovations*, 2nd edition, Washington, D.C.: Georgetown University Press, 2008.

Giles, Keir, *Russia's "New Tools" for Confronting the West: Continuity and Innovation in Moscow's Exercise of Power*, London: Chatham House, The Royal Institute of International Affairs, March 21, 2016. As of August 13, 2017: https://www.chathamhouse.org/publication/russias-new-tools-confronting-west

Goble, Paul A., "Defining Victory and Defeat: The Information War Between Russia and Georgia," in Svante E. Cornell and S. Frederick Starr, eds., *The Guns of August 2008: Russia's War in Georgia*, Armonk, N.Y.: M. E. Sharpe, 2009.

Gordon, Michael R., "NATO Commander Says He Sees Potent Threat From Russia," *New York Times*, April 2, 2014. As of August 15, 2017: http://www.nytimes.com/2014/04/03/world/europe/nato-general-says-russian-force-poised-to-invade-ukraine.html

Grabo, Cynthia M., *Anticipating Surprise: Analysis for Strategic Warning*, Bethesda, Md.: Center for Strategic Intelligence Research, Joint Military Intelligence College, 2002.

———, "Soviet Deception in the Czechoslovak Crisis," *Studies in Intelligence*, Vol. 14, No. 1, Spring 1970, pp. 19–34.

———, "The Watch Committee and the National Indications Center: The Evolution of U.S. Strategic Warning 1950–1975," *International Journal of Intelligence and Counterintelligence*, Vol. 3, No. 3, 1989.

Grady, John, "EUCOM Emphasis Shifting to Russian Deterrence," *USNI News*, July 14, 2016. As of August 14, 2017: https://news.usni.org/2016/07/14/u-s-european-command-shifting-russian-deterrence-missions

Graham, Bob, Jim Talent, and Graham T. Allison, *World at Risk: The Report of the Commission on the Prevention of WMD Proliferation and Terrorism*, New York: Vintage Books, 2008.

Gressel, Gustav, *Russia's Quiet Military Revolution, and What It Means for Europe*, European Council on Foreign Relations, 2016.

Grove, Thomas, "Russia Says It Is Creating Three New Divisions to Counter NATO Moves," *Wall Street Journal*, May 4, 2016. As of August 14, 2017:

http://www.wsj.com/articles/russia-says-it-is-creating-three-new-divisions-to-counter-nato-moves-1462360562

Hall, Steven L., "Why the West Should Pay More Attention to Moldova," *Stratfor*, February 20, 2016. As of August 14, 2017: https://www.stratfor.com/weekly/why-west-should-pay-more-attention-moldova

Handel, Michael I., "The Yom Kippur War and the Inevitability of Surprise," *International Studies Quarterly*, Vol. 21, No. 3, September 1, 1977.

Harris, Shane, "Washington's Civil War over Russia Intel," *Daily Beast*, October 12, 2015. As of August 12, 2017: http://www.thedailybeast.com/articles/2015/10/12/washington-s-civil-war-over-russia-intel.html

Herb, Jeremy, "Clapper: Ukraine Was Not an Intelligence Failure," *The Hill*, March 10, 2014. As of August 14, 2017: http://thehill.com/policy/defense/200322-clapper-ukraine-was-not-an-intelligence-failure

Heuer, Richards J., Jr., *Psychology of Intelligence Analysis*, Washington, D.C.: Central Intelligence Agency, Center for the Study of Intelligence, 1999. As of August 13, 2017: https://www.cia.gov/library/center-for-the-study-of-intelligence/csi-publications/books-and-monographs/psychology-of-intelligence-analysis/PsychofIntelNew.pdf

Heuer, Richards J., Jr., and Randolph H. Pherson, *Structured Analytic Techniques for Intelligence Analysis*, Washington, D.C.: CQ Press College, 2010.

Hicks, Kathleen H., Heather Conley, Lisa Sawyer Samp, Jeffrey Rathke, Olga Oliker, and Anthony Bell, *Evaluating Future U.S. Army Force Posture in Europe: Phase I Report*, Center for Strategic and International Studies, February 2016. As of August 14, 2017: csis.org/files/publication/160203_Hicks_ArmyForcePosture_Web.pdf

Illarionov, Andrei, "The Russian Leadership's Preparation for War, 1999–2008," in Svante E. Cornell and S. Frederick Starr, *The Guns of August 2008*, Armonk, N.Y.: M. E. Sharpe, 2009.

Jervis, Robert, "Why Intelligence and Policymakers Clash," *Political Science Quarterly*, Vol. 125, No. 2, June 2010.

Johnston, Rob, *Analytic Culture in the U.S. Intelligence Community: An Ethnographic Study*, Washington, D.C.: Central Intelligence Agency, Center for the Study of Intelligence, 2013.

Kalb, Marvin, "Putin's Deceptive Pause: What Are Russia's Next Steps in Ukraine?" Brookings Institution, September 1, 2015. As of August 14, 2017: https://www.brookings.edu/blog/order-from-chaos/2015/09/01/putins-deceptive-pause-what-are-russias-next-steps-in-ukraine/

Kam, Ephraim, *Surprise Attack: The Victim's Perspective,* Cambridge, Mass.: Harvard University Press, 1988.

Kaža, Juris, and David Gauthier-Villars, "Latvia's Wariness over Russia Raises Civil Rights Concerns at Home," *Wall Street Journal*, August 26, 2016. As of August 14, 2017: http://www.wsj.com/articles/latvias-wariness-over-russia-raises-civil-rights-concerns-at-home-1472246717

Kendall, Bridget, "What Next for President Putin?" *BBC News*, December 31, 2015. As of August 14, 2017:
http://www.bbc.com/news/world-europe-35198486

Kringen, John A., "Rethinking the Concept of Global Coverage in the U.S. Intelligence Community," *Studies in Intelligence*, Vol. 59, No. 3, September 2015.

Kulesa, Lukasz, "Towards a New Equilibrium: Minimising the Risks of NATO and Russia's New Military Postures," European Leadership Network, Policy Brief, February 8, 2016. As of August 14, 2017:
http://www.europeanleadershipnetwork.org/towards-a-new-equilibrium_3497.html

MacEachin, Douglas, *Predicting the Soviet Invasion of Afghanistan: The Intelligence Community's Record*, Washington, D.C.: Center for the Study of Intelligence, 1999.

Masters, Jonathan, "How Strong Is the Russian Military?" *Newsweek*, December 12, 2014. As of August 12, 2017:
http://www.newsweek.com/how-strong-russian-military-291366

McCarthy, Mary O., "The Mission to Warn: Disaster Looms," *Defense Intelligence Journal*, Vol. 7, No. 2, 1998.

———, "The National Warning System: Striving for an Elusive Goal," *Defense Intelligence Journal*, Vol. 3, 1994.

McCreary, John F., "Warning Cycles," *Studies in Intelligence*, Vol. 27, No. 3, Fall 1983.

Mehta, Aaron, "Gen. Breedlove: Intelligence Community Changing How It Handles Russia," *Defense News*, October 30, 2015. As of August 11, 2017:
http://www.defensenews.com/story/defense/policy-budget/budget/2015/10/30/intel-community-russia-breedlove/74867614/

Miller, Greg, "As Russia Reasserts Itself, U.S. Intelligence Agencies Focus Anew on the Kremlin," *Washington Post*, September 1, 2016. As of August 12, 2017:
https://www.washingtonpost.com/world/national-security/as-russia-reasserts-itself-us-intelligence-agencies-focus-anew-on-the-kremlin/2016/09/14/cc212c62-78f0-11e6-ac8e-cf8e0dd91dc7_story.html?utm_term=.b43e0ddf4e7e

Ministry of Defense of the Russian Federation, "Severny i Baltiiski floty v ramkakh vnezapnoi proverki boevoi gotovnosti narashivaiut sostav sil v akvatoriiakh Barentseva i Baltiiski morei," February 27, 2014. As of August 15, 2017: http://function.mil.ru/news_page/country/more.htm?id=11905692

———, "Voiska (sily), zadeistvovannye v proverke boevoi gotovnosti perebrasivaiutsia v aznachennye raiony," February 27, 2014. As of August 15, 2017: http://function.mil.ru/news_page/country/more.htm?id=11905614

Monaghan, Andrew, *Russian State Mobilization: Moving the Country on to a War Footing*, London: Chatham House, The Royal Institute of International Affairs, May 2016.

National Commission on Terrorist Attacks Upon the United States, *The 9/11 Commission Report: Final Report of the National Commission on Terrorist Attacks Upon the United States*, New York: W. W. Norton & Company, 2004.

Norberg, Johan, *Training to Fight: Russia's Major Military Exercises 2011–2014*, Swedish Defense Research Agency (FOI), November 2015.

Office of National Estimates, *The Military Buildup in Cuba*, Special National Intelligence Estimate Number 85-3-62, September 19, 1962.

Patton, Thomas J., "The Monitoring of War Indicators," *Studies in Intelligence*, Vol. 3, Winter 1959, document declassified on September 18, 1995 (part of Record Group 263 in "Records of the Central Intelligence Agency, 1894–2002," National Archives at College Park, Md.). As of August 13, 2017: http://research.archives.gov/description/7283404

Pherson, Randall H., "The Tradecraft of Warning: Overcoming Cognitive Barriers," paper prepared for Seminar on the Tradecraft of Warning: New Approaches and New Thinking, hosted by the ODNI's National Intelligence Council and the U.S. State Department's Bureau of Intelligence and Research, February 20, 2009.

"Press Conference by NATO Secretary General Jens Stoltenberg Following the Meeting of the NATO-Ukraine Commission at the Level of Defence Ministers," North Atlantic Treaty Organization, June 15, 2016. As of August 14, 2017: http://www.nato.int/cps/en/natohq/opinions_132488.htm

"Press Conference by President Obama after NATO Summit," The White House, Office of the Press Secretary, July 9, 2016. As of August 14, 2017: https://www.whitehouse.gov/the-press-office/2016/07/09/press-conference-president-obama-after-nato-summit

Recommendations of the Jeremiah Report, Washington, D.C.: National Security Archive, George Washington University, MORI Doc. ID 406297, June 2, 1998. As of August 13, 2017: http://nsarchive.gwu.edu/NSAEBB/NSAEBB187/IN38.pdf

Roberts, James Q., *Maskirovka 2.0: Hybrid Threat, Hybrid Response*, MacDill Air Force Base, Fla.: Joint Special Operations University Center for Special Operations Studies and Research, Occasional Papers, December 2015.

Science Applications International Corporation, *Warning in Uncertainty—Rethinking Warning in a Changing World*, conference summary, Herndon, Va., February 1, 2000.

Serebryannikov, V. V., "Thoughts on the Concept of 'War,'" *Voyennaya Mysl*, October 1, 2004.

Shlapak, David, and Michael W. Johnson, *Reinforcing Deterrence on NATO's Eastern Flank: Wargaming the Defense of the Baltics*, Santa Monica, Calif.: RAND Corporation, RR-1253-A, 2016. As of August 11, 2017: https://www.rand.org/pubs/research_reports/RR1253.html

Smith, Michael Douglas, "The Perils of Analysis: Revisiting Sherman Kent's Defense of SNIE 85-3-62," *Studies in Intelligence*, Vol. 51, No. 3, 2007. As of August 14, 2017: http://connection.ebscohost.com/c/articles/73468169/perils-analysis-revisiting-sherman-kents-defense-snie-85-3-62

Snegovaya, Maria, *Putin's Information War in Ukraine: Soviet Origins of Russia's Hybrid Warfare*, Washington, D.C.: Institute for the Study of War, Russia Report I, September 2015.

Steury, Donald P., ed., *Sherman Kent and the Board of National Estimates*, Washington, D.C.: Central Intelligence Agency, Center for the Study of Intelligence, 1994.

Thomas, Timothy L., "Russia's Reflexive Control Theory and the Military," *Journal of Slavic Military Studies*, Vol. 17, 2004. As of August 13, 2017: https://www.rit.edu/~w-cmmc/literature/Thomas_2004.pdf

Tilghman, Andrew, "EUCOM Commander: US May Need to 'Puncture' Russian Defenses," *Defense News*, March 1, 2016. As of August 14, 2017: https://www.defensenews.com/global/europe/2016/03/01/eucom-commander-us-may-need-to-puncture-russian-defenses/

U.S. European Command, *U.S. European Command Posture Statement 2016,* February 25, 2016. As of August 14, 2017: http://www.eucom.mil/media-library/article/35164/u-s-european-command-posture-statement-2016

"US Intelligence Lapse on Russian 'Surprise' Moves in Syria Probed," *Newsmax*, October 8, 2015. As of August 14, 2017: http://www.newsmax.com/TheWire/us-intelligence-russia-syria/2015/10/08/id/695210/

Whaley, Barton, *Stratagem: Deception and Surprise in War*, Norwood, Mass.: Artech House, 2007.

The White House, *The National Security Strategy of the United States*, September 2002.

———, *The National Security Strategy of the United States*, March 2006.

———, *The National Security Strategy of the United States*, May 2010.

———, *The National Security Strategy of the United States*, February 2015.

Wilson, Andrew, *Ukraine Crisis: What It Means for the West*, New Haven, Conn.: Yale University Press, 2014.